# LEADING
## with

## Sage Advice From
## 100 Experts

Jann E. Freed

ASTD
PRESS

**ASTD Press** is an internationally renowned source of insightful and practical information on workplace learning, performance, and professional development.

ASTD Press
1640 King Street Box 1443
Alexandria, VA 22313-1443 USA

**Ordering information:** Books published by ASTD Press can be purchased by visiting ASTD's website at store.astd.org or by calling 800.628.2783 or 703.683.8100.

Library of Congress Control Number: 2013942806

ISBN-10: 1-56286-870-5
ISNB-13: 978-1-56286-870-3
e-ISBN: 978-1-60728-751-3

**ASTD Press Editorial Staff:**
Director: Glenn Saltzman
Manager and Editor, ASTD Press: Ashley McDonald
Community of Practice Manager, Workforce Development: Ron Lippock
Editorial Assistant: Sarah Cough
Text and Cover Design: Natasha van de Graaff, Marisa Kelly, and Lon Levy

Printed by Versa Press, Inc., East Peoria, IL, www.versapress.com

# Praise for This Book

"There are leadership practices and there are leadership practices, but not all of them matter. Jann Freed, in her relentless research over several years, has gathered the wisdom, insights, and practices of leaders she has identified as 'sages,' and has distilled from all that material the things that really matter in leadership. I only wish I'd had this book when I was a young manager trying to be a leader. Read this, then give a copy to every aspiring leader you know, as well as to those who are in leadership positions but haven't figured out yet what really matters."

**Jim Autry**
Author of *The Servant Leader* and *Choosing Gratitude*

"*Leading With Wisdom* is a welcome addition to the thinking of millions of Boomers who are at the turning point of their generational life: from leading the pack of doing to leading the pack of reflecting. This book will help today's 55-75 year olds support the generations we are mentoring. No matter where you fall in the spectrum of professional life, Jann Freed's thoughtful research and stories will inform and inspire."

**Christina Baldwin**
Author of *Storycatcher: Making Sense of our Lives through the Power and Practice of Stories* and *The Circle Way: A Leader in Every Chair* (with Ann Linnea)

"Through enlightening interviews and wise commentary, Jann Freed reveals the secrets of great leadership and shows us a path to purposeful sage-ing. A profoundly relevant book for every leader today."

**Richard Leider**
Author of *Repacking Your Bags* and *The Power of Purpose*

"This book is exactly what we need to find our way during this chaotic and troubling time. Other cultures have always relied on wisdom keepers—those elders who have lived with awareness and discernment. It's time for us to realize that we cannot survive without such wisdom—wisdom that is always simple, clear, and eternally true."

**Margaret J. Wheatley**
Author of many books, most recently: *So Far From Home: Lost and Found in Our Brave New World*

"If you read the business headlines, it is easy to believe that wisdom is sorely lacking in our leaders and organizations, and that it is desperately needed. It is true that greater wisdom is desperately needed. And this book is full of wisdom from leadership sages, wisdom you can use immediately in your own leadership, because it's been there in you all along. It is a book of hope and inspiration. Jann Freed's stories and research give you the courage to live your deepest principles and to embrace these eight powerful, meaningful and effective leadership practices. We all need to be living in alignment with these, wherever we show up. That would be heaven on earth."

**Judi Neal**
Author of *Edgewalkers: People and Organizations that Take Risks, Build Bridges, and Break New Ground* and *Enlightened Organizations: Four Gateways to Spirit at Work*

"I can easily recommend Jann's book as it is a vote for restoring our humanity. This is much needed in this instrumental world, especially among those concerned with leadership. The book is also written with a light and flowing touch which offers the ideas in a very accessible way."

**Peter Block**
Author of *Flawless Consulting: A Guide for Getting Your Expertise Used* and *Community: The Structure of Belonging*

*In loving memory of*
*Dr. Elmer Burack—Sage, mentor, and dear friend*

# Table of Contents

# Foreword

Over the course of my lifetime, I have had the good fortune to enjoy some extended time with a few men and women who have lived extraordinary lives. It was during those times that my curiosity drove me to ask them as many questions as I could think of as to how they came to do what they were able to do that contributed to them becoming who they were known to be. From time to time, I have wondered what it would be like if I could invite them to come together and share their stories in such a manner that I could capture the common emerging themes. It was and still is my belief that such an experience would not only be life enriching, but most likely life changing.

Jann Freed's book, *Leading With Wisdom*, has accomplished what I have been wishing for, particularly as it relates to the somewhat mysterious subject and practice of leadership. Not only was she able to track down some of the wisest people (sages) who have something significant to say about leadership, but she has identified the common themes emerging from the conversations that she had with these sages. As a long-time student of leadership, I will ever be grateful to Jann for patiently persisting over nearly a decade to not only capture these nuggets of wisdom, but to present them in a form that encourages me to apply them to my own life, as both a leader and as a consultant to leaders who desire to make a positive difference in the world.

I encourage all who pick up *Leading With Wisdom* to pace their reading in such a way that would allow sufficient time and space to ask themselves how each of the eight leadership practices are being lived out in their own lives, and maybe even following up with what changes might be considered. I personally believe that any meaningful read is a dangerous read since it can often lead to the consideration of making some type of personal change. I believe that for many, *Leading With Wisdom* will be such a book, if taken seriously and applied to one's own life. To the extent that each of us approach this book as a learner, the more likely that our investment in time and money will prove to be one of the better investments that we will make, as evidenced by the positive impact that we will have on the lives of those within our sphere of influence.

Raymond Rood
Founding CEO and Senior Consultant
The Genysys Group

# Preface

L*eading With Wisdom* is a book that takes a practical yet holistic approach to the topic of leadership. It challenges all leaders—including frontline managers, departmental and divisional leaders, as well as upper management and CEO-level leaders—to evaluate and even benchmark their current approach to leadership against the practices identified by some of the world's most successful leadership experts, gurus, and top organizational leaders and CEOs. This is a book that invites the reader to learn how these experts and leaders have tapped into their own hard-won job experiences and life lessons to truly discover what it means to be a connected, engaged, and successful leader.

Since curiosity drives research, I was curious about how to be the most effective leader and how to best prepare people to be the kinds of leaders needed in these uncertain times. Eventually my research expanded beyond my original intention. In the end, this book is an integration of the concepts drawn from the literature, from the numerous thought leaders I interviewed—I call them "sages"—into a personal quest to live what I was learning.

Sages are people who are able to synthesize life experiences and translate them into wisdom that is shared with others as part of their legacy work.

In addition, I interviewed senior leaders of organizations that had received an award for creating healthy workplaces that encourage and support people in bringing their minds, bodies, and spirits to work. I am certified as a Sage-ing© Leader, Registered Corporate Coach,® Change Management Consultant, and attended several workshops and seminars with important thought leaders. The culmination of these experiences informed my thinking and my journey to learn how to be an effective leader in an uncertain and chaotic world.

So my personal journey became action oriented—following the advice and wisdom of the sages. Whatever I was learning along the way, I integrated into my courses, workshops, and life. This book explains a leadership philosophy and the practices that evolved from my active pursuit of listening and putting what I heard into action. This involved engaging in the activities they advocated, reading the materials they recommended, and developing practices they felt essential for leading and living a quality life. But this was the surprise: When I asked the sages about leadership—they told me about life.

The themes that emerged from this learning journey form the heart of this book. A key lesson (perhaps even confirmation) was that the best leaders are highly self-aware, generous, empathetic, compassionate, and they truly understand the power of building community by sharing what they know. This is just one of the broad lessons I learned through a nine-year interview project that grew to include talks with more than 100 respected thought leaders and dozens of other renowned leadership "sages" and experts, from Warren Bennis, Peter Senge, Stephen Covey, Sally Helgesen, Marshall Goldsmith, Shoshana Zuboff, Jim Kouzes, Daniel Pink, Patricia Aburdene, Peter Block, Margaret Wheatley, Jim Autry, and Max De Pree. *Leading With Wisdom* helps those in positions of authority follow this lead and intentionally use all of their life experiences—as an organizational, team, or workgroup leader, as a community member or leader, as a family member, or just individual experiences—to support and inform the job of inspiring others to succeed. In short, this book helps leaders integrate the best of themselves and their lives into the tasks and roles of leaders.

As a teacher and researcher focused on the nature and practice of leadership, I find that most theories and models of leadership are too simplistic for the complexities of today's organizations and environments. Those with the responsibility to lead others seem to be drowning in information about the nature and practice of leadership, all the while starving for wisdom about what behaviors nurture the people and organization they serve and support. This book is intended to cut through this excessive information to offer leaders simple ways to positively move their careers and their lives forward.

While I did not initially plan to write a book, my curiosity about how to best prepare people to be leaders led me on a life-changing journey—one that has no end. The Spanish poet Antonio Machado wrote a poem that seems to reflect the journey I have been on for years in seeking wisdom and learning about leading. It is called "Proverbios y Cantares" (Proverbs and Songs) from his book *Campos de Castilla (Fields of Castile, 1907-1917)*, and this excerpt reflects my journey:

*"Caminante, no hay camino. El camino se hace al andar."*
*Walker, there is no path. The path is made by walking.*
—Antonio Machado

Jann Freed

# Acknowledgments

This has been a learning journey—one on which I did not know where the path was leading. I just kept walking and learning along the way. I am grateful to the people, organizations, and circumstances that enabled me to go on this quest of seeking wisdom from leadership sages. I want to thank:

Central College. When I started this research project, "In Search of Sages," I was on sabbatical as a professor of business management and the Mark and Kay De Cook Endowed Chair in Leadership and Character Development. The college financially supported my professional development through conference and workshop participation. This participation helped me interview many of the sages personally. The endowed chair helped me purchase the materials I needed to record telephone interviews with most of the sages.

Mark and Kay De Cook. With the support of the endowed chair provided by the De Cooks, this project has forever changed my life. I am honored to have Mark and Kay as friends.

Judi Neal. At the time I started this project, Judi was the director of the International Center for Spirit at Work, where she conducted teleconferences with authors and leaders of organizations that had received an award for "spirit at work." It was a privilege for me to help Judi interview many of these people who I then interviewed as sages in my study.

Elmer Burack. I would not have started on this journey without the encouragement and insightful wisdom of Elmer. He was the impetus and his spirit kept me going.

More than 100 sages. Thank you to each and every person I interviewed. Each interview was a learning experience that I can share with others in a variety of ways—this book, my blog, articles, and in courses and workshops. I am forever grateful for the life experience and wisdom you shared with me.

Mark Morrow and Ashley McDonald. After a 30-year career in higher education, it was a challenge for me to break from "academic speak." Thank you for helping me find my own voice and coaching me with your thoughtful feedback.

John Fisher and sons. Writing a book is a commitment of time and energy. And I realize there are opportunity costs when I am focused on a project such as this. Thank you for understanding and supporting me in the process. Since I am passionate about learning, I hope what I learn benefits my relationships as well. This book has taught me about living one's best life and my life is best because all of you are in it.

# Chapter 1

## Introduction to the Eight Practices

*In a few hundred years, when the history of our time will be written from a long-term perspective, it is likely that the most important event historians will see is not technology, not the Internet, not e-commerce. It is an unprecedented change in the human condition. For the first time—literally—substantial and rapidly growing numbers of people have choices. For the first time, they will have to manage themselves. And society is totally unprepared for it.*

*—Peter Drucker*

Years ago, I was mesmerized by Mary Catherine Bateson's book, *Composing a Life* (1989). In the book, Bateson, an anthropologist who is the daughter of Margaret Mead and Gregory Bateson, examines the lives of several accomplished women with interesting, multifaceted careers, and concludes their success was the result of the unifying thread of their varied experiences and their effective use of it. *Leading With Wisdom* is intended to help leaders of all kinds do just that—use their life experiences for success. And "success" for a leader—whether it's of an organization, team, workgroup, community, or family—is to support others and inspire them to succeed.

This book offers those working in all types of organizations—and at all levels—the key concepts and applications for expanding how they use their leadership and life skills repertoire. The content is based on several unique factors including:

- concepts drawn from interviewing more than 100 leadership sages—thought leaders in the field

- themes distilled from reading books and articles recommended by the sages interviewed

- ideas and concepts collected from interviewing numerous senior leaders of award-winning organizations

- personal experiences with leadership from my career and life.

## Eight Leadership Practices That Matter

With such a wide variety of leaders, I assumed that narrowing down key insights would be difficult, but that was not the case. After analyzing the data and other research, eight "sage-worthy" practices emerged that underpin leaders who connect with and inspire others to achieve high performance. Specifically, my research revealed the following characteristics (after which I named each chapter of the book). Leaders:

- know who they are

- don't let ego win

- connect with empathy and compassion

- admit mistakes fearlessly

- embrace community

- create healthy work environments

- live their legacy.

## Who Should Read This Book?

The specific audience for this book includes anyone in a position of influence in organizations (profit and not-for-profit) or those who train these individuals, specifically frontline managers, departmental and divisional leaders, as well as upper management and CEO-level leaders. It offers these professionals a way to evaluate and even benchmark their current approach to leadership against the practices identified by some of the world's most successful leadership experts, gurus, and top organizational leaders and CEOs. This book invites readers to learn how these experts and leaders have tapped into their own work experiences and life lessons to truly discover what it means to be a connected, engaged, and successful leader.

As the late sage Peter Drucker intuitively pointed out: "We are in one of those great historical periods that occurs every 200 or 300 years when people don't understand the world anymore, and the past is not sufficient to explain the future" (Cameron and Quinn, 1999, 1). But as the world changes, human relationships become even more important.

This is a lesson I learned on my journey and I incorporated it into my own personal life as well. In addition, I developed workshops and leadership courses at the undergraduate and graduate level based on the lessons learned in the process of writing this book. I have been on a quest to learn how to lead and to live from people with rich life experience.

# Sage as Leader

As an investment counselor, my husband's role model and mentor from afar is Warren Buffett. One of our rituals is to attend the Berkshire Hathaway annual meeting in Omaha and I am always struck by the thousands of people who attend. Many of them come from around the world to be in the presence of Buffett and Charlie Munger, who is Buffett's partner and vice chairman of Berkshire Hathway.

Buffett is often quoted as saying, "Learning how to live is much more important that learning how to make a living." Buffett carefully scrutinizes the people who hold leadership positions in every business he purchases. Berkshire's philosophy is that they are investing in the current management who get to continue running their business. His goal is to keep them and not to replace them. So he needs to know and understand the people well.

Buffett is also known for sharing his wisdom with several MBA classes every year. The students either travel to Omaha or he travels to the institution. He often starts off by saying, "I'm here to talk to you all about anything and everything you want, whether it is personal, political, or business in nature." One of his messages has to do with what he looks for in a manager or leader and he repeatedly says the same four things: passion, intelligence, energy, and integrity. And he says if they don't have integrity, he would prefer to have them "dumb and lazy because they will do less damage."

Even though Buffett is an investor, people want to probe his life experiences about all kinds of topics, such as education, happiness, fear, trust, retirement, love, relationships, and death. In fact, he discourages his top managers from retiring by telling them that Mrs. B. (Mrs. Blumkin, former CEO of Nebraska Furniture Mart) died one year after she retired (at age 103). Buffet believes that you need to have a reason to get up in the morning, and why not continue doing something you love as long as you can do it?

Buffett and Munger are known for "cutting to the chase" and focusing on what is most important. For Buffett, what is essential has to do with living one's best life. He realizes that leadership and business are based on quality relationships. It is hard to have quality relationships with people who lack integrity and with whom trust is not possible.

One story that made an impression on me had to do with friend-ships. Buffett knows a woman who survived a concentration camp, but she was slow to make friends because she wondered if they would "hide her." So Buffet uses the "Would they hide me?" test in determining who is a real friend.

---

## How to Get the Most From This Book

*Leading With Wisdom* describes how to integrate the eight key leader-ship practices into your life as a manager, other organizational leader, or learning professional. It backs up this promise with a practical application at the end of each chapter that details ways to integrate the concepts that have been discussed into everyday practice or training program planning. In addition, each chapter features several sidebar examples that illustrate the main points. The end of chapter section also provides specific techniques that help the reader further develop and continue the practice highlighted in the chapter.

## "There You Are"

In ancient cultures, a group's sages were those who had experienced rich lives, were thoughtful about what they had learned through these experiences, and willingly shared them with others. As Jon Kabat-Zinn so wonderfully outlines in *Wherever You Go There You Are* (2000), mountain climbing is a powerful metaphor for the "life quest, the spiritual journey, the path of growth, transformation, and understanding." In mountain climbing, before moving up the mountain to the next encampment, you must replenish the camp being left for the people who will come after you; and when returning, go down the mountain a ways to share with the other climbers the knowledge gained from farther up the slope.

"As best we can, we show others what we have seen up to now. It's at best a progress report, a map of our experiences, by no means the absolute truth. And so the adventure unfolds. We are all on Mount Analogue together. And we need each other's help," says Kabat-Zinn.

This book is my way of sharing what I have learned as I have climbed the "mountain." I want to share the knowledge and wisdom gained so that others may benefit from my journey.

## Chapter-by-Chapter Description

Each chapter concludes with Workshop and Personal Development Suggestions as examples of how to integrate the concepts into your life (or into a new or existing training or learning program). Reading suggestions are also included for further personal development.

## Chapter 1: Introduction to the Eight Practices

The introduction outlines how the book is organized, who should read the book, and how to get the most from the book. The eight practices of connected, engaged, and successful leaders are briefly described along with the unique factors on which they are based.

## Chapter 2: Leaders Know Who They Are

Knowing who you are involves more than recognizing strengths and weaknesses. This chapter offers some specific ways to discover what motivates and informs how and why you choose to lead others. Specific techniques are offered to help you discover these motivations. Also included are ways other leaders have taken this journey of self-discovery. Readers can take lessons from the experiences of these other leaders.

## Chapter 3: Leaders Don't Let Ego Win

This chapter explores the origins of ego and argues for a healthy understanding and use of our ego. Without this understanding, the dark side of a leader's ego often emerges, creating a toxic environment. Learning to let go in order to move on is critical. Included are specific practices on keeping the ego in balance.

## Chapter 4: Leaders Connect With Empathy and Compassion

Empathy and compassion are often considered soft skills, but the consistent practice of these skills is anything but soft. This chapter explains why it is essential for leaders to understand some basic concepts of loss, death, and grief in order to have empathy and compassion for life's many transitions—including loss of jobs, position, power, and purpose at work and at home.

## Chapter 5: Leaders Admit Mistakes Fearlessly

Admitting mistakes fearlessly is a characteristic of effective leaders, and it includes self-forgiveness and the forgiveness of others. Admitting mistakes allows others to trust us. We trust others more easily as well. The winner in this trust dance is the organization and all those who work in a healthy, open environment.

## Chapter 6: Leaders Embrace Community

Organizations are systems of interconnected parts, just as the communities in which we live. The best leaders are social architects working to build high-functioning organizations, but the work is not easy to finesse. This chapter discusses this community concept and how managers and other leaders can use this connection with community in their organization and in their own community where they live to become more effective managers and leaders.

## Chapter 7: Leaders Model Resilience

Leaders need to model resilience and renewal in order to thrive through uncertainty and lead in chaos. This chapter outlines how a true sense of curiosity and creative thinking are essential for effectively modeling a resilient attitude and mindset.

## Chapter 8: Leaders Create Healthy Work Environments

Leaders have an absolute obligation to create healthy work environments. This chapter includes specific examples of how award-winning organizations and their leaders built healthy, productive work environments and repaired toxic ones.

### Chapter 9: Leaders Live Their Legacy

Leaders create their legacy every day and the epitaph is written daily with the decisions they make, how they make them, and the way those affected are treated along the way. This chapter discusses the concept of "living legacy" and the transformational potential of approaching leadership in this holistic way.

### Chapter 10: Final Thoughts

This last chapter summarizes the main lessons that formed the framework for this book and includes some specific conviction and beliefs about the life of a leader.

## What's Next?

Self-knowledge is the touchstone for every successful leader. The next chapter helps you develop a more reliable sense of yourself and what motivates and nurtures you. It also provides significant insight into seamlessly incorporating this self-knowledge into your work as a leader and daily challenges as a member of your family and community.

# Chapter 2

# Leaders Know Who They Are

*The journey of our lives is to discover.*
—*Margaret Wheatley*

One of my favorite techniques to engage and challenge leaders attending my courses and workshops is to pose a simple, direct question: *Would you follow yourself?*

For me, those who are capable of answering this question honestly are well on their way to becoming extraordinary leaders. Peter Drucker, the father of modern management, wrote extensively about self-management. He clearly understood that leaders, or anyone else for that matter, cannot exist separately from their internal values and beliefs.

Dozens of other thought leaders, practitioners, and other assorted sages I have interviewed over the years have repeatedly confirmed Drucker's insight into what grounds and sustains great leaders. That endorsement reinforces why there are so many self-assessments used by consultants and leadership trainers that are specifically designed to help leaders align their inner and outer values, beliefs, and motivations.

Still, after interviewing more than 100 authorities in the field— whom I refer to as leadership sages—I am convinced that a deeper, more powerful level of self-knowledge is possible; an insight that pushes and challenges the best leaders to acknowledge and confront what they fear most, with the reward being even greater success in their work and private lives. These are the leaders who work the hardest to peel away their vulnerabilities and insecurities as one might disassemble a Russian nested doll—matryoshka or babushka. Because the work is scary, many leaders have not engaged in it because it takes them far out of their comfort zones. However, for leaders such as Jim Autry, Parker Palmer, Peter Senge, Peter Block, Margaret Wheatley, Sally Helgesen, Christina Baldwin, and others noted in this book, it's difficult work that is richly rewarded. Ray Rood, the founder and CEO of The Genysys Group, said it this way, "Becoming a leader and becoming an adult are mysteriously interconnected."

Dr. J.-Robert Ouimet is chairman of the board and chief executive officer of Holding O.C.B. Inc., Cordon Bleu International Ltd., and Piazza Tomasso International Inc. Ouimet was already a successful leader when he met Mother Teresa. Yet, the encounter changed his life. He told me that after spending time with her (at least four times in Calcutta), he was determined to live his life differently. In fact, he shared with me his transformative story:

> "The first time I met Mother Teresa, I told her I only had one question for her. 'Should I give everything I have away?' It took her four minutes to answer. Then she said, 'You have nothing to give. Nothing is yours. It has all been loaned to you. Together with God, you can manage what has been loaned to you. Manage everything first for your spouse, followed by children, and then each person working in your company—really His company.'

*"After spending two days with Mother Teresa in Calcutta,
I came home and made changes in my own behaviors and
started new practices in the workplace, such as creating a
'silence room' for contemplation, reflection, and prayer."*

# Mindful Leadership Practice

Mindful leadership is learning to "achieve nothing." Introducing such a possibility to business colleagues can be a lot fun because it rouses such passion and, at times, disdain. The entire notion seems so upsetting—so insultingly counterintuitive—that to be an inspiring leader we need to not accomplish, not achieve, not succeed. Yet, while such a suggestion as "achieving nothing" may seem utterly inappropriate, the practice of mindfulness points out in no uncertain terms that to lead a dignified life and to lead others well, we must perfect the effort of non-achievement (Carroll, 2012a, 127).

## The Rewards of Becoming a Reflective Leader

Many of us, including a great number of leaders, believe that productivity and being "busy" are somehow directly connected. Nothing could be further from the truth. Doing is different from being, and the best leaders are introspective leaders who are adept at being while doing, which is a skill that takes a long time to develop. One sage said, "We need to remember we are human beings, not human doing." These leaders practice a pragmatic mindfulness that allows them to learn and grow as a leader and person (see the sidebar on the previous page).

A mindful approach is vastly different from more regimented approaches that focus on shifting or adjusting personality traits and styles to become better leaders—although these are often valid pathways to gaining an understanding about an individual leader's motivations and drives. Many of the leaders I interviewed at some point in their careers completed personality assessments (such as MBTI, Strengthfinders, DiSC) and no doubt learned a great deal from the exercise; perhaps they even used the insights they gained to enhance their leadership capabilities.

Slowly the concept of mindfulness is finding its way into business leadership institutions. The Drucker School of Management and Wharton Business School offer instruction in mindfulness meditation as a leadership development discipline. Companies such as Aetna, Merck, General Mills, and Google all are exploring how mindful meditation can help their leaders and employees embrace and thrive in today's extremely competitive and fast-paced business environment (Carroll, 2012b).

Bob Atchley, author of *Social Forces and Aging*, said in our interview that it was only after he began developing a more mindful, connected approach to his work that he felt truly happy and successful. Atchley described mindfulness as an intentional way of life. One goal is to be connected to our spiritual core in order for "clarity, compassion, and aliveness" to emerge in our life's work. Another goal is to rise above ego-centered thoughts and behaviors. "It is not possible to manifest sage qualities from an ego-centered consciousness."

# This Is Water

There are these two young fish swimming along and they happen to meet an older fish swimming the other direction who nods at them and says, "Morning boys. How's the water?" And the two young fish swim on for a bit, and then eventually one of them looks over at the other and says, "What the hell is water?"

The immediate point of the fish story is merely that the most obvious, ubiquitous, important realities are often the ones that are the hardest to see and talk about. In the 20 years since my own graduation, I have come gradually to understand these stakes, and to see that the liberal arts cliché about "teaching you how to think" was actually shorthand for a very deep and important truth. "Learning how to think" really means learning how to exercise some control over how and what you think. It means being conscious and aware enough to choose what you pay attention to and to choose how you construct meaning from experience. It is about the real value of a real education, which has nothing to do with grades or degrees and everything to do with simple awareness—awareness of what is so real and essential, so hidden in plain sight all around us that we have to keep reminding ourselves over and over, "This is water. This is water."

Source: Wallace, D.F. (2009). *This Is Water: Some Thoughts, Delivered on a Significant Occasion, About Living a Compassionate Life.* New York: Little, Brown and Company.

Peter Senge, the author of the groundbreaking book *The Fifth Discipline: The Art and Practice of the Learning Organization* (1994) and co-author of *Presence: Human Purpose and the Field of the Future* (2004), calls this state of being *presencing*, a combination or blend of the words "presence" and "sensing." Senge defines this state as "an inner place from which leaders operate." Senge says that leaders can only achieve this through a shift of mind, shift of will, and shift of heart.

Judi Neal, chairman of Edgewalkers International, said it this way: "There is too much emphasis in leadership development on educating people in the head and not enough about their hearts— compassion, values, integrity, and forgiveness. Leaders need to learn to take care of themselves—mind, body, and spirit."

According to Russ Moxley, author of *Leadership and Spirit: Breathing New Vitality and Energy Into Individuals and Organizations* (2000), "Leadership needs to go beyond the what and how to under-standing the who of the leader by going on a deep inner journey."

## Changing Is Difficult Work

Clearly, this is difficult work; especially when doing (even unpro-ductive doing) is rewarded—a least in the short term—and being still remains a "nice work if you can get it" concept. That's unfortu-nate, because people behave in ways that are rewarded. Think of the overwhelming activity when the individual snowflakes in a snow globe after you shake it up (imagine the flakes swirling around the Washington Monument or the Eiffel Tower). It is only when all of the snowflakes all settled on the bottom—at the end of activity—that you are able to clearly see what is inside. A "quiet," free-of-chaos mind thinks more clearly. Without clarity, we can't be effective. Wise leaders make thoughtful decisions that come from being grounded, and this is a vantage point of differentiation from other leaders.

Parker Palmer, author of *Let Your Life Speak*, reinforced the value of practicing mindfulness in order to be grounded. He told me that leaders are "constantly falling into an ego trap or hall of mirrors that is a web of illusions and delusions." Because of this, we need to pay more attention to the inner life of the leader.

In my workshops, I often encourage this "mindful" approach using a technique I learned from Richard Leider. I ask the group two questions and ask the participants to shout the answers back to me.

Q: "What time is it?"

A: "Now."

Q: "Where are we?"

A: "Here."

If the class is ongoing or continues for multiple days, I ask these two questions at the beginning of every class (see this activity and a few variations on it at the end of this chapter). What's interesting is that if I forget to perform the ritual for recurring classes, it is the participants who remind me of the oversight. I think the leaders really "get it" when this happens. Some students and workshop participants have even told me that they have made this statement their personal mantra, repeating it every time they find themselves seeing more "snowflakes" than clear, clutter-free insight.

## The Problem With Multitasking

In simple terms, mindfulness is the opposite of mindlessness; especially in our multitasking age that focuses on checking items off the "to do" list without considering what is important or most productive. Stephen Covey's book, *First Things First* (1994) with Roger and Rebecca Merrill, certainly was a direct acknowledgement of this simple truth, but it's not a lesson that most of us have learned. However, for leaders, it's a way of being that is vitally important.

Jim Collins, author of *Good to Great* (2001) and *Great by Choice* (2011) advises us to keep a "to learn" list instead of the standard "to do" list as a way to focus on learning. Collins also advocates a "stop doing" list because there are only 24 hours in a day. If we are going to learn something new, what are we going to stop doing to make time for this new activity? This also helps us focus on what matters most.

As Meg Wheatley explained to me, "We have to know who we are in order to be grounded in ethics and personal identity." Busyness can be numbing rather than awakening. It's hard to imagine any-one—especially leaders—who would consciously consider busyness as productivity. Yet, that's where many leaders end up unless they stop and take time to consider a new approach.

## Personal Mindful Connections

For me, one pathway to a more "mindful" way of living—the practice of yoga—came as a result of doing the research for this book. After a few months of practice, it occurred to me that many commonly used yoga terms had a remarkable connection to mindful leadership practices (some of these terms are listed in a chart on the following page).

While several of the sages mentioned practicing yoga as a way to feel grounded, other practices used to connect with the inner self in-cluded meditation and journal writing. Any pathway to get beyond fear to be open and create space for clarity can be considered a mindful prac-tice. For André Delbecq, the McCarthy University Professor at Leavey School of Business, Santa Clara University, meditation is a pathway: "People such as me who practice stillness meditation seek to 'transcend' the ever roaming 'monkey mind' caught in repetitive and sometimes compulsive cycles of consciousness, to step away from the superficial ego's preferences and desires, and to enter into an inner quiet."

## Common Terms for Mindful Leadership Practice

| Balance | Process | Acceptance | Spirit |
|---|---|---|---|
| Vision | Reflection | Compassion | Listen |
| Journey | Groundedness | Practice | Connection |
| Core | Flexibility | Strength | Expanded |
| Energy | Detachment | Purpose | Intention |
| Quiet | Letting Go | Mindfulness | Fear |
| Breath | Centered | Deliberation | Conscious |
| Emotion | Silence | Nonjudgmental | Embrace |
| Movement | Presence | Envision | Pause |

Christina Baldwin, author of *Storycatcher: Making Sense of Our Lives Through the Power and Practice of Story* (2005), was a founder of the journal-writing movement. It's how she accesses her "inner quiet." She told me that for her "developing a practice such as journaling, in which we consistently turn life experience into the story of what is happening, provides a sense of deep internal organization to how I behave in the course of a day."

## Slowing Down

Learning to be present and fully aware may sound simple or even doable, but as noted, neither our society nor our workplaces are supportive of "slow down" approaches. In fact, we're encouraged to do just the opposite. That's why I include a certified yoga instructor in my leadership classes to lead a session on the basic techniques and practices of yoga. I share some basic techniques here, but you'll find an expanded exercise suitable for personal use—or for use in any larger learning events such as workshops or seminars—at the end of the chapter.

One of the first concepts taught in yoga is the significance of the breath. Since we have conscious control over the breath, we are able to maintain control and balance. While we can't control the heartbeat, we can alter our patterns of breathing, which gives us conscious control over the rest of our bodies and helps us become self-aware, while at the same time relieving stress and increasing our ability to focus. Some other techniques include:

- **Embrace simplicity:** Let go of the desire to be preoccupied; allow yourself to slow down; be at ease with what arises in your daily experience and appreciate it.

- **Embrace process:** The journey and the work, not the destination or the success, is the treasure.

- **Embrace listening:** Tune into others with your ears rather than your voice; be open, aware, and inviting of all the messages coming from others and your surroundings.

## The Power of Silence

In this culture in which we live and work, being silent and seeking silence is another way of slowing down. It is in silence that we can listen to our inner voice and wisdom. Through silence, we are able to focus on being present; clearly a difficult state to achieve in our normal, everyday life. For me, my silent time is at a monastery in

Dubuque, Iowa called the New Melleray Abbey. But there are other ways you can seek needed silence and solitude, including workshops and seminars that include long periods of silence. In fact, anything we can do to break habits of thinking can be a good practice.

J.-Robert Ouimet finds time at a monastery for a weekend retreat every two months to clear his mind. When I asked him about this, he had this response: "Everything starts with silence. Silence leads to prayer and prayer leads to faith. Faith leads to love and love leads to compassion and service. This leads to peace and peace leads me back to silence. When I am in silence, I can discover who I am. And there are many ways to be in silence in order to stop the mind and open the heart."

Any regular physical exercise such as running, walking, or biking is as good for the mind as it is for the body. Jim Autry, former president of Meredith Corporation Publishing Group, walks daily to clear his head before the day begins. Engaging in any repetitive movements help us break out of our patterns so new thinking and behaviors can emerge.

There are many empirical studies documenting results of stillness meditation. "These include physiological changes in brain and neurological functioning; health outcomes including immune deficiency improvement; quicker recovery from illness or injury; enhanced ability to deal with pain; lower blood pressure; and greater access to restorative sleep. There are also psychological and affective outcomes: a growing ability to listen; less need to dominate; patience with others and irritating circumstances; greater focus; less anxiety; increased optimism; less cynicism; greater self-confidence; and an overall higher perceived quality of life" (Delbecq, 2012, 9).

In addition to yoga, there are many examples of activities to encourage focus and slowing down. Thai chi, drumming, dancing, meditation, prayer, and journaling are a few methods of altering our state of consciousness so that we get beyond thinking and beyond fears. Activities that enable us to break free and stop our thinking, help us to pay attention to our intuition, put us in touch with our bodies, and move us away from judgment are valuable for leadership and personal development. In my workshops, I also incorporate drumming as an activity to help open the mind to new possibilities (see the example at the end of this chapter). As confirmed by Dan Petersen, an executive coach whom I interviewed at his retreat center in Sage Canyon, Colorado: "Creative breakthroughs," he said, "often emerge during repetitive exercises."

## The Power of Purpose

What was most clearly revealed in my research is something we already know—even if we don't acknowledge it. We are all searching for a sense of purpose and meaning. New research shows "there is a strong correlation between happiness and meaning. … When we cultivate mindfulness and meaning in all that we do, including our work, we have the opportunity to influence not only our own well-being, but also the well-being of our family, friends, coworkers, and wider community" (Dishman, 2013). Richard Warren's bestselling book, *The Purpose Driven Life* (2002) is evidence of this basic human desire. As executive coach and author Richard Leider says to those who attend his seminars or work with him one-one-one, "What is your reason for getting up in the morning?"

Howard Behar is the former president of Starbucks Coffee Company International and the author of *It's Not About The Coffee:*

*Leadership Lessons From a Life at Starbucks* (2007). Behar expressed the importance of leaders this way: "Before you can do something, you must first be something. We need a purpose bigger than ourselves. My purpose is to nurture and inspire the human spirit. I start with myself and then work to do this with others. That's how I want to live my life and how I want to be remembered."

## Bottom Line

The bottom line is that it's hard to be an inspiring leader and breathe life into people if you are not clear on your own purpose, vision, mission, and values. Richard Leider conducted research in conjunction with the MetLife Mature Life Institute and produced a report titled *Discovering What Matters: Balancing Money, Medicine, and Meaning* (January, 2009). Interestingly, the report focused on those between the ages of 45 and 74. The findings included:

- Regardless of age, gender, financial status, or life stage, the majority of people assign the most importance to meaning-related activities such as spending time with friends and family.

- People with a sense of purpose in their lives are more likely to report being happy and describe themselves as living the "Good Life."

Leider makes it clear in this study and in his writing that living the "Good Life" is not just about material wealth and physical comfort, but "living in the place you belong, with the people you love, while doing the right work on purpose." The bottom line of the study was this: *Meaning trumps money and significance trumps success.*

This finding certainly supports what many of the thought leaders and gurus consistently told me in interviews. Below are a few of the validations from these individuals that mirror the MetLife bottom-line results.

Jim Autry, not only a sage, but also a neighbor and friend told me how critical it is to nurture our inner life: "This means doing anything that stimulates you to expand your thinking and encourage you to become more reflective. It means letting go of the left brain or rational part and being more open to a sensual way of taking in the world. This is deep interior work. For me, this work informs how I behave and affirms what I do as well as my personal growth."

Another sage, Darlyne Bailey, co-author of *Sustaining Our Spirits: Women Leaders Thriving for Today and Tomorrow* (2008), put it this way: "The most effective organizational and community leaders have to be doing their own inner work. I could never lead and help others become healthy if I didn't work at it myself. Leaders have to be doing their own self work—just as the best teachers have to keep learning." Another example comes from David Campbell, creator of the Campbell Interest and Skill Survey (CISS). He told me that his inner work has been done through more than 30 years of journaling. "Spiritual growth comes from reading where one has been."

## Mindful Presence in the World

Purpose is directly connected to how mindful and present we are in the world. It is hard to know what we are all about and what is important to us if we are not working and living in the present. We can't practice discernment if we are not awake. At the end of my workshop with Pema Chodran, author of *The Places That Scare You: A Guide to Fearlessness in Difficult Times* (2005) and a leading proponent of the power of being present, she closed the workshop by saying: "Get out of your own way. Let things unfold. Cherish the wonder. Feel the magic. Surrender to the big picture. And remember, the lighter you are, the happier—loosen the grip. Each 24 hours is an opportunity to awaken rather than reinforce bad habits."

One of my favorite company tag lines is provided by Caribou Coffee Co. At least on its coffee cups, this is an organization that has already figured out the power of presence and purpose: "Life is short," the tagline proclaims, "Stay awake for it."

## Implementing the Practice

Robert "Skip" Backus, CEO of the Omega Institute of Holistic Studies, reminded me that "A practice is something that can't be taken away. It is a constant source of information and opens up intuition," and that is critical for making the best decisions. Leaders need to cultivate a healthy state of mind and not be distracted by anxiety and fear. Then we are more capable of listening and expressing ourselves with more authenticity and a greater sense of inner peace.

When we have a practice that grounds us, we have an inner compass that frees us from the domination of our "dark side" or "shadow" that often manifests itself as fear, anxiety, greed, jealousy, and hubris. These behaviors create toxic environments for everyone working within them. This topic will be explored in more detail in the next chapter, "Don't Let Ego Win."

What follows is a wide variety of ways you can begin (or continue) the work of self-discovery as the first stop on your journey to become a more connected, engaged, and successful leader. While I am not suggesting you personally do each of the exercises every day or use them all in any one learning event, it is important to develop a practice, and you can choose which practice most appeals to you.

Regardless how you decide to proceed, you must engage and follow through—and you must challenge those just learning the power of these concepts to engage and follow through—in order to get any true benefit from these concepts and grow as a leader. If you'd like to see some examples or would like further references, you can go to the associated website for this book, www.jannfreed.com/Leadingwithwisdom.

## Workshop Suggestions

### 1. What Time Is It?

*Description:* This exercise has many uses and not just for leadership classes. The purpose is to drive home the point of being present and in the moment. You can use it to just encourage engagement with your participants. You don't have to put the prompt in your PowerPoint presentation or write it on a flip chart, but there's nothing wrong with doing that.

*Instructions:* You ask the questions and the participants say the answers in unison. I use this as a chant—repeating the questions two to three times and having participants answer. I often mix up the order of the questions just to make sure participants are listening and paying attention—which is the point of the exercise.

Q: "What time is it?"

A: "Now."

Q: "Where are we?"

A: "Here."

### 2. Breaking Free

*Description:* This exercise can be used as an excellent grounding exercise. While the concept sounds simple, the act of paying attention to breathing can have a powerful impact.

*Instructions:* Tell your participants to envision the breath as a rope that is tethering them to the ground. Pay attention to your breathing.

Just notice the breath as it enters the body. Slow it down. Deepen it. Notice how it calms you down. When you feel overwhelmed, upset, or confused, pay attention to your breathing—counting to 10 and paying attention to each inhalation will calm your mind, body, and spirit. It gives us a time to regroup, to rethink about the moment, to decide what to do next. Where do we want to put our attention? What thoughts do we want to have?

### 3. Mindful Eating

*Description:* The point of this exercise is to make people pay attention to what they are eating.

*Instructions:* Mindful eating seems counterintuitive in a fast-food society. This exercise allows participants to practice mindfulness with taste. Bring something flavorful (such as chocolate, strawberries, bagel pieces and cream cheese) for each participant and explain about the importance of being aware and intentional about every aspect of life, including eating.

After passing out your chosen food to the participants, note that when we are mindful, we recognize what we are picking up and examine the food. The focus is on thinking about what we are doing, what we are eating, and how it tastes.

Ask questions such as: How was this experience different from normal eating? How did you feel during this exercise? How many times do we eat and not even remember what we ate or how it tasted?

### 4. Mindful Traveling

*Description:* This exercise is to make people pay attention regardless of how they are traveling.

*Instructions:* Mindful traveling, whether walking, driving, or biking, helps us be fully aware and connected to the world around us. Tell participants to imagine changing one of their regular traveling routines. Ask questions such as: How did it feel to take this new path? What did you notice? What difference might this new awareness of surroundings make in your life?

## 5. Sitting Meditation

*Description:* This exercise will help you and your participants in a learning event sit down and be still in order to cultivate being patient, open, and humble.

*Instructions:* Begin by sitting upright; relaxed, but awake. Keep your eyes open with your gaze slightly downward. Put your hands with palms down gently resting on the thighs. Your face and jaw should be relaxed. Breathe normally and sit still. Your senses should become alive and you will notice what you are thinking. When this happens, label it "thinking" and return your attention back to your breath. The purpose is to "let go" of your emotions and thoughts. Imagine them as a balloon you have let go into the air and they are floating away.

## 6. Listening Exercise

*Description:* This exercise is to make us aware of how hard it is to truly listen and for others to feel heard.

*Instructions:* Listening is a critical aspect of being present, awake, and in the moment. Since listening is an important leadership and interpersonal skill, I often read passages from books on a variety of topics in seminars, workshops, and classes so people can practice active listening while learning aspects of the topics such as mindfulness. Reading aloud is good for any age. Select passages that are relevant to the workshop content. Before reading, ask people to take a breath to get grounded and prepared for listening.

7. **Silence Exercise**

*Description:* The purpose of this exercise is to sit in silence to become centered and focused on being present.

*Instructions:* At the beginning of each class, workshop, or meeting, sit in silence for one to two minutes. Explain that this is the time to "empty" out the mind to "be open to receive" new information. You can use this ritual of silence between agenda items or workshop topics.

## Personal Development Suggestions

1. **Journaling**

*Description:* This exercise is to practice writing down thoughts and feelings.

*Instructions:* Journaling helps you find your leadership center in many ways. First, it keeps you reflecting on your life experiences and helps you make connections that support your personal growth. Journaling also provides insights you often are unable to access in any other way. You may find your "ah-ha" moment as you write, or the insight might come as you review your entry later.

However you gain this insight does not matter as long as the effort helps you realize that you need to change course to achieve your goals, or continue on the path you're on, or just make slight adjustments. Many who are dedicated to journaling advocate using paper and pen to record their reflections and thoughts, but if you're more comfortable using a keyboard, that's fine too. You can create a private blog online that you can access from anywhere, or create a secure cloud-based document (Google Docs, for example). It doesn't matter how you do the work since the rewards to your leadership development will be the same. You don't have to be profound or clever. Your job is to explore your thoughts in an open and honest way. The focus is the process of understanding your inner dialogue.

As noted, you don't have to use pen and paper. Examples of free online options if you prefer to keep your journaling in the cloud are http://penzu.com and http://www.my-diary.org.

### 2. Life Review

*Description:* This activity is similar to journaling (you might even make it a part of your journaling exercise), except that this is a direct effort to capture the arch of your life for review and contemplation. The point of the exercise is to discover "who you've been" to help you define "who you will (or want to) become." Søren Kierkegaard, the Danish philosopher, famously said, "Life is lived forward, but understood backward."

*Instructions:* How you approach this exercise depends on your energy, time, and talents. Don't worry about the form or how well you are able to express yourself. Think of the exercise as a creative, free-form resume if that helps you get started. For example, you might begin by simply stating something such as:

*I've always been interested in how things work. Even when I was a kid I jumped at the chance to take things apart—toys, broken toasters, just about anything. That's maybe why I ended up working in the auto industry.....*

Or, if you don't think you can do a narrative, you might simply describe each of your jobs and how you moved from one to the other, or what you learned doing each that is helping or hurting your development toward meeting your goals. You might even take a Facebook Timeline approach to this exercise and list major life events—defining moments—and career moves down a page (paper or digital) filling in important details about your life.

Take a few minutes now to consider how you'd like to approach this exercise, then set up the initial template that you'll use (narrative, timeline, or another method of your choosing). If possible, begin telling the story of your life now; or set aside a specific time to devote to this exercise.

Christina Baldwin uses a modification of the life review exercise. She advocates that people write a story about themselves in third person because it helps their life purpose emerge. To begin the story, start with the statement: *Once there was a man (or woman) who …*

### 3. Find Silence and Solitude

*Description:* This exercise will help you be intentional about finding silence and solitude.

*Instructions:* Where can you find peace and quiet? This can be as simple as taking a walk in nature or going on a bike ride. Don't use musical devices. Listen to nature. Listen to your inner voice.

### 4. Get Some Feedback

*Description:* One way to decrease your "blind spots"—those aspects of yourself and your behaviors that others see but we do not see—is to get honest feedback. Sometimes answering direct questions can give you keen insight as to what motivates and drives the decisions you make.

*Instructions:* You can take this exercise on as a solo exercise, answering the questions below in narrative form for your eyes only. Or, you might want to ask a close friend or colleague to listen to your answers and provide feedback and follow-up questions. If you choose to involve someone else, you might trade roles and get in a little practice in the art of listening.

Below are some sample questions to use, but you can add others as appropriate:

- What sustains you as a leader?

- What threatens you?

- What would you want to share with leaders to come?

- During your early years, which people had the greatest impact on you?

- Starting with your earliest memories, what have been your defining moments?

- What have been your highs and lows as a leader?

- What would you want to change about yourself to become more effective?

An alternate or additional approach might be to create a personal advisory council, basically a group of people you can call upon for feedback, advice, and wisdom. It does not have to be a group that meets together, but they have agreed to serve you in this way.

### 5.  Practice Mindfulness, Find Silence and Solitude, Breathe

*Description:* The point of all these exercises and techniques is to help you find and listen to your inner voice; the one that often will lead you in the right direction if you're willing to listen. Some might call it your "gut instinct," but the idea is the same. We all have the ability to "know" when something is right. You just have to know when and how to listen.

As noted earlier in this chapter, mindfulness is all about paying attention to the moment; the now of life. Being mindful means really thinking about what we are doing, whether it's eating, walking on a country road, or breathing. Try this little breathing exercise to get a feel for the experience.

*Instructions:* Envision the breath as a rope that tethers you to the ground. Notice the breath as it enters and exits your body. Try slowing your breathing down. Increase the volume of breath. If you do this, you'll notice a definite calming effect. That's why we often tell someone who is upset or overwhelmed to "breathe, breathe." The best leaders are able to think clearly and remain calm in the midst of even the most stressful situations. That's why being a mindful leader is so important.

## 6. Daily Meditative Messages

*Description:* Subscribe to a daily meditative message sent to your email account (such as www.dailyom.com) or notes to inspire (such as www.startwithwhy.com) where the focus is on cultivating mindfulness, inspiration, and well-being in the workplace. Every weekday, DailyOM sends inspirational thoughts for a happy, healthy, and fulfilling day. It's free. This is a good way to keep focused on what matters most. The messages are spiritually based and a daily reminder of the value of staying grounded. Madisyn Taylor has compiled two books based on her inspirational messages (*DailyOM: Inspirational Thoughts for a Happy, Healthy, and Fulfilling Day* and *DailyOM:*

*Learning to Live*, published by Hay House, Inc.). These messages can be read to start your day. They can also be shared at the beginning of a meeting or class to get the audience in the right frame of mind.

## Readings

While there are many excellent resources on these topics, a few favorites are Ellen Langer's books *Mindfulness* (1989), *The Power of Mindful Learning* (1997), and her more recent book *Counterclockwise: Mindful Health and the Power of Possibility* (2009). Michael Carroll writes extensively about mindfulness for leaders such as in *The Mindful Leader: Awakening Your Natural Management Skills Through Mindfulness Meditation* (2007). Eckhart Tolle's *The Power of Now* (1999) and his more recent book, *A New Earth* (2005), are classics on presence. The essence of Tolle's message is condensed in his book *Stillness Speaks* (2003).

A classic article I use in leadership workshops is from *Harvard Business Review* (July-August, 1992) titled "Parables of Leadership." It consists of several leadership parables in which the lessons are timeless.

## What's Next?

The next chapter explores ego development and argues for a healthy understanding and use of our ego. Without this understanding, the dark side of a leader's ego often emerges, creating a toxic environment. Learning to let go in order to move on is critical. Included are specific practices on keeping the ego in balance.

# Chapter 3

# Leaders Don't Let Ego Win

*If you're looking over your shoulder, you can't have much vision.*

—Jim Autry

One of the most common themes of leadership development is that leadership begins with self-knowledge and developing personal insight about individual strengths and abilities. So it is ironic to consider that the same strengths that might make leaders successful could be the leading cause of their downfall. Of course, most leaders understand this balancing act. That's why so many leaders participate in seminars for leaders, attend various leadership institutes, and read so many books on the topic (if leadership bestseller lists are any measure). This, of course, begs the question, why are there so many bad leaders?

In the *Journal of Management Inquiry,* André Delbecq wrote an article titled "Evil Manifested in Destructive Individual Behavior: A Senior Leadership Challenge." He defined the evil individual as someone who "sucks the life juices from the organizational group by unusually destructive behavior, crippling the group in such a way that all positive spirit is lost." In the article, Delbecq explains how most people in organizations are not prepared to deal with "evil" individuals. While people who demonstrate deeply hurtful behavior are usually rare, they do exist, and they create toxic environments for others in the organization. Delbecq said he wants to believe that most leaders desire to be good bosses and that their behavior is the result of being unaware of their own leadership blind spots.

So much of what it takes to excel as a leader has to do with self-management—knowing who you are at a deep level—and how you use this knowledge and awareness to build relationships. Working America, a community affiliate of the AFL-CIO, sponsors an annual event called "My Bad Boss Contest" (www.workingamerica.org/bad-boss). The event offers an opportunity for workers to speak out about the difficulties they face on the job. Workers are encouraged to share an anonymous story about a nightmare boss for a chance to win a well-deserved, week-long vacation.

I have shared these stories in a variety of settings—with students and workshop participants—as illustrations of the dark side of leadership. It's unfortunate that just a small amount of self-knowledge and acknowledgement of leadership blind spots is all that is needed to solve most of the problems the employees share on the website. In fact, Margaret Wheatley told me, "People in my audiences describe their workplaces as 'land of the walking dead.'"

If bad bosses were not so common, people would not relate to a movie titled *Horrible Bosses* with Jennifer Aniston. As a result of being such a popular movie, there is talk of a sequel. Similarly, it is no surprise that a television show such as CBS's *Undercover Boss* is so popular; the premise is that the boss gets an opportunity to work in the position of an employee and gain a new and enlightening perspective on what it's like to "walk in the shoes" of employees.

My favorite definition of leadership was from a workshop I attended facilitated by Peter Senge, author of *The Fifth Discipline: The*

*Art and Practice of the Learning Organization* (1990). Senge asked us to come up with different words for "leader"; people mentioned words such as "inspiration" and "aspiration." He reminded us that *spire* comes from the Latin root meaning literally "breath" or "breath of life." Therefore, he defines leadership as the ability to "breathe life into someone or something." I have modified this slightly for my work: Leaders breathe life into people, programs, and projects. If leadership is about breathing life into people, places, and projects, then the toxic air created in organizations as a result of poor leadership habits and skills is a productivity killer, which will eventually extinguish the life of even the best and most engaged employee.

James Hunter, author of *The Servant: The Simple Story About the Essence of Leadership* (1998), reminded me that it is not about moving up to the level of leader, but about the end of the journey—being an effective and good leader. One of the main questions, Hunter told me, is: "Are people better off because we are their leaders?" Sadly, this is not true in many cases because ego and narcissism win the day.

## Understanding the Ego

Many of our corporate leaders are selected for the wrong reasons. The trend in leadership has been toward the hero leaders who are charismatic and placed on a pedestal by followers. They are charismatic, but lack character. They have style, but they lack substance. They are highly profiled, but lack integrity. The dark side of this model is leaders' fear of showing vulnerability by displaying any weakness, imperfection, or insecurity. Often these fears are masked in excessive pride that expresses itself as arrogance, a sense of entitlement, difficulty accepting responsibility for mistakes, and addiction to perfection. "Leaders do not need to know all of the answers. They do need to ask the right questions"—even of themselves (Heifetz and Laurie, 1997, 124).

In his book, *The Paradox of Success: When Winning at Work Means Losing at Life* (1993), John O'Neil states that "successful people struggle with shadows especially in the areas of money, power, relationships, and responsibilities" (36). Since leadership involves all of these components, a clear theme of the sages was to be on the lookout of the downside of success and don't let the ego win. O'Neil came to the conclusion that "the single greatest danger of success is that it encourages us to overlook or discount the darker sides of ourselves" (51).

My research revealed that understanding ego development should be part of leadership development. Understanding the ego is essential for gaining some initial insight into what motivates and drives leaders, and it's an essential insight needed to understand your own leadership motivations. So much of leadership involves initiating, leading, and sustaining change, and the ego can enhance or inhibit change efforts. "Invested in ego, we defend against change. Divested of ego, we work cooperatively toward change" (Richo, 1999, 43).

Dan Petersen, an executive coach, shared this definition of ego with me during a four-day retreat I attended in Colorado at a facility that he interestingly named Sage Canyon: "The ego is the difference between what you want to have happen and what is happening. It is the gap between what we want and what is. When we learn to 'let go' of the difference, we are controlling the ego and not letting it control us."

Petersen said there are levels of development, and it is a process of moving from "it's all about me, to it's all about us, to the very inclusive, it's all about all of us." Ego development is the critical component for leadership development. Petersen explained how he works to help leaders develop.

> *"I help leaders realize the principle that you can't get enough of what you don't need; where the ego plays into that principle is that it always wants more. More money, more admiration, more success, and that drives us into thinking we need to go outside of ourselves to get what we need. In that way, the dark side of materialism comes into our lives, diverting us from sufficiency and what is really needed is to live life almost intuitively from our true nature, which Richard Leider calls living from the inside out. A materialistic mindset can corrupt too easily the idea that something outside of ourselves can bring happiness and success."*

Angeles Arrien explained to me that she believes it is important to differentiate between letting be and letting go. She said they are two processes that challenge us every day to accept things as they are, especially during times of change. In her book, *Living in Gratitude* (2011), she says, "The state of letting be requires us to increase our levels of trust and acceptance of what is occurring in the moment, without pushing or holding back to attempt to create a different experience. Letting go is a willingness to release, in the moment, what might impede our progress. When we sense resistance in letting go, this may be a signal where we are overly attached or controlling" (189).

Michael Carroll, author of *The Mindful Leader* (2007) and *Awake at Work* (2004), explained the ego this way: "When we think of 'ego,' we often think of a 'thing' or a psychological 'identity,' which is understandable given how we often speak about the Freudian approach to personality. In Buddhism, however, 'ego' is no 'thing' or identifiable psychological structure. Rather, 'ego' is a deeply ingrained set of habits that keep us constantly misunderstanding our situation."

Essentially, "ego" is our attempt to secure ourselves in a world that offers no guarantees; and consequently, we end up in a complex and painful enterprise to make sure that "I am going to be ok." But since we can never get such reliable assurances, we spend our time constantly checking, trying to make sure—"Am I going to be ok? Is this going to work out?" Since we never get the needed reassurance, we become frustrated, angry, frightened, and impoverished as we fail over and over again. This entire enterprise of seeking false reassurance and all the confusion, pain, and insanity it causes is "ego."

In my interview with David Richo, he explained how he uses the acronym FACE to describe the shadow side of the ego, and how we need to understand how it has a positive and creative side. Richo describes FACE in detail in *Shadow Dance: Liberating the Power & Creativity of Your Dark Side* (1999, 50):

> "The F for fear becomes an acknowledgement of our vulnerability while contacting the excitement on the other side of fear. Then we find ourselves acting bravely with fear but not because of it. The A of attachment becomes bonding in a committed but nonpossessive way. The C for control becomes power for not over others. The E for entitlement becomes speaking up and standing up for our rights self-nurturantly but then letting the chips fall where they may. "Each feature of the FACE of ego causes pain. Fear is first because it is the origin of the other three and because it may have happened first in our lives. We attach because

*we fear loss. We control because we fear grief. We demand
entitlement because we fear the condition of existence
that warns us things are not always fair. There is a higher
power than the scared-child ego. It is the adult power of
ourselves that can work a program of change, such as this
book presents. The higher power spiritually is the grace that
shifts us into transformation. Work on letting go of ego is
ultimately a spiritual practice. "*

Parker Palmer has written a great deal about the impact of the
dark side of leadership. Palmer puts it this way in *Let Your Life Speak:
Listening for the Voice of Vocation* (1999): "A leader is someone with
the power to project either shadow or light onto some part of the
world and onto the lives of the people who dwell there. A leader
shapes the ethos in which others must live, an ethos as light-filled as
heaven or as shadowy as hell. A good leader is intensely aware of the
interplay of inner shadow and light, lest the act of leadership does
more harm than good."

Jack Gibb, in his classic book *Trust* (1978), describes a fear-
distrust cycle—one where "a self-fulfilling prophecy ensues: low-trust,
high-fear theories generate more fear and distrust." He concludes that
fear is the opposite of trust and that fear and distrust always go together and often lead to defensiveness. And defensiveness is one main way
the dark side likes to manifest itself. "This vicious defense cycle occurs in organizations particularly when fears are high and at times of
emergencies, poor market conditions, pressure from top management,
cultural unrest, labor pressures, heightened ambiguity, or massive
change of any kind." He writes that the cycle "spirals and feeds upon
itself" and "builds a general climate of constraint; creates dependent,

passive and conforming people, and brings such people into positions of visibility and influence—the Peter principle; and sets up forces and organizational structures that sustain the fear of defense" (192).

David Foster Wallace was invited to speak to the 2005 graduating class of Kenyon College and his commencement address became a classic after his death, and was even published in a book, *This Is Water: Some Thoughts, Delivered on a Significant Occasion, About Living a Compassionate Life* (2009, 98-113). He warns us all about the power of ego:

> "In the day-to-day trenches of adult life, there is actually no such thing as atheism. There is no such thing as not worshipping. Everybody worships. The only choice we get is what to worship. ... If you worship money or things—if they are where you tap real meaning in life—then you will never have enough. Never feel you have enough. It's the truth. Worship your own body and beauty and sexual allure and you will always feel ugly, and when time and age start showing, you will die a million deaths before they finally plant you. ... Worship power—you will feel weak and afraid, and you will need ever more power over others to keep the fear at bay. Worship your intellect, being seen as smart—you will end up feeling stupid, a fraud, always on the verge of being found out. And so on. Look, the insidious thing about these forms of worship is not that they're evil or sinful; it is that they are unconscious. They are default settings".

The sages I interviewed noted over and over how critically important it is to understand ego development to prevent good leaders from going bad. Leaders who are unaware of this dark side often are the worst leaders who create the most destructive and toxic work environments.

In *Bad Leadership: What It Is, How It Happens, Why It Mattters* (2004) author Barbara Kellerman makes recommendations for minimizing bad leadership behaviors that result from all too human characteristics of greed, defensiveness, and micromanaging. Her advice includes:

- *Share power:* Working alone increases the chance leaders will lose touch with reality and abuse the power they have earned.

- *Don't believe your own hype:* When we hear something repeatedly, we tend to believe it, whether it is true or not.

- *Compensate for weakness:* Leaders should be willing to admit what they can't do or don't know and find people who can and do.

- *Get authentic:* Healthy skepticism either from the leader or advisers goes a long way toward keeping leaders grounded.

- *Stay balanced:* Leaders need to live a holistic and healthy life in order to make thoughtful and effective decisions.

- *Be reflective:* Self-insight requires continual reflection in order to learn and not repeat the same mistakes. Know who you are.

When leaders realize that continuous quality improvement (CQI) is personal, then they seek feedback that can keep the dark side from taking over. Though it is easier to focus on the positive aspects of leadership development, it is essential for us to understand our shadow side so we do not move to the dark side. In order for this to happen, we need to realize the process starts with being committed to continuously learning, growing, and becoming the kind of leader others will follow. Just ask yourself the question, "Would you follow yourself?"

# Four Human Drivers

In *Driven: How Human Nature Shapes Our Choices* (2002), Paul Lawrence and Nitin Nohria identify four primary innate drivers that they believe are hardwired in the brains of all humans. These drivers shape the choices we make; Lawrence and Nohria base their contention on four critical assertions.

First, the four drivers are innate and universal. Second, they are independent, but highly interactive with each other. Third, the drivers are not derived from one another or from a single underlying mental drive. Finally, the four drivers are a complete set. While similar to Maslow's hierarchy of needs, these authors emphasize that each of the drives has a positive side and a negative side, which they refer to as the "dark side" of the drive. When the drives are not in balance, unhealthy behaviors are displayed. Each drive must be satisfied. Your job as a leader is to keep them in balance.

- *Driver 1:* The first (D1) is the *drive to acquire* objects and experiences that improve our status relative to others.

- *Driver 2:* The second (D2) is the *drive to bond* with others in long-term relationships of mutually caring commitment.

- *Driver 3:* The third (D3) is the *drive to learn* and make sense of the world and of ourselves.

- *Driver 4:* The fourth (D4) is the *drive to defend* ourselves, our loved ones, our beliefs, and resources from danger.

Lawrence and Nohria conclude that those who have found ways to satisfy all four drives (at least over time) will feel more fulfilled than those who have focused on some to the exclusion of others. The key to success is to keep the drives in balance so that your ego stays in check.

When you neglect the drive to acquire, you are more likely to lack self-esteem and feel envious of those who have done better. When you neglect the drive to bond with others, you are apt to feel empty and disconnected from life. When you neglect the drive to learn and instead have lived a life with little opportunity to pursue our own curiosities, you are more likely to feel stunted in your personal development. When you neglect the drive to defend or have been unable to do so, you are more likely to feel used and victimized.

Interestingly, strengths that are too strong become weaknesses. For example, someone who is a great public speaker, charismatic, and excellent at networking is often a poor listener. These individuals have been rewarded for their strengths and are often unaware of their weaknesses. When you are aware of your shadow side, you are open to feedback and you put systems in place to obtain honest input and understand the value of surrounding ourselves with those who complement our strengths.

While we need to have an ego, it needs to be a healthy ego—and an ego in balance. Healthy leaders create healthy workplaces for themselves and for others. When we lack an understanding of ego development, it is difficult to demonstrate compassion and empathy or understand how we might be contributing to a toxic work environment.

## Letting Go of Ego

One way of overcoming the dark shadow side of leadership is learning to "let go" of the fears that affect our success and happiness. Five of the biggest shadows to overcome are insecurity; competition in response to a culture of perceived hostility; overdeveloped responsibility and the belief that we can fix or control everything; denial of death, or the refusal to acknowledge the death of ideas and things that are no longer working; and fear, especially the fear that we will be viewed as failing. When we face our shadow, "we are better able to shed light on our organizations that they need for growth rather than to suffocate them in darkness" (Bailey, et al., 2008). Without learning how to detach from negative emotions, the dark side of the ego can take over; but doing so takes courage—takes heart. In fact, it takes courage to be authentic, particularly in organizations that are dysfunctional or even toxic.

The concepts discussed in this chapter are well known, and some institutions are actively working toward solutions. One way of letting go is to create different kinds of organizations. Kim Cameron of the University of Michigan told me his institution had created a new field of study called Positive Organization Scholarship. Essentially, a positive organization emphasizes appreciation, abundance, collaboration, and vitality over greed, dishonesty, winning, and gaining personal wealth, as the road to a healthy organization. The result of this positive focus is an organization that spends its time sharing wisdom, being generous, building social relationships, demonstrating compassion, and practicing forgiveness.

Robert Sutton, author of *Good Boss, Bad Boss* (2010), says that if a workplace is mired in meanness, it is likely the boss deserves part of the blame and may not even realize it. People who have power often have no idea of their impact on others. They don't know how their weaknesses are hurting morale and performance. It is true that there are a few "bad apples" in some workplaces. But if leaders think about the legacy they are leaving on a daily basis, the odds are good that they will be considered good bosses and casting more light than darkness in the workplace.

Leaders don't ever arrive at being the perfect leader—or even person, for that matter. As leaders, if we discover our strengths, are aware of our dark side (and we each have one), and consistently think about the legacy we are leaving with our decisions and behaviors, then we should be creating an environment where people want to work.

So how do you—or those you train, coach, or mentor—develop these valuable organizational and life skills? This is an area where work is needed for most people who influence the lives of others. What follows are a wide variety of ways you can begin (or continue) to build the attributes of a leader who refuses to let ego win.

Since fear plays a key role in feeding the dark side or shadow, there are also exercises in chapter 4 that will be helpful. Some of the exercises that follow can be used personally or in a workshop setting. Again, I am not suggesting you personally do each of the exercises every day or use them all in any one learning event. You should choose which practice or approach moves you forward in your career and life.

## Workshop Suggestions

### 1. The Two Sides of the Ego

*Description:* This exercise makes us aware that there are two sides of the ego.

*Instructions:* While we are aware that we have an ego, we may not understand the two sides of the ego. The goal is to help people differentiate between the two sides in order to develop a healthy ego. As the two lists of descriptors are read, ask participants: Where do you stand today and how can you move to the left side of the list?

| Healthy Ego | Neurotic Ego |
|---|---|
| Observes | Denies or dissects |
| Assesses | Judges and blames |
| Learns from mistakes | Repeats old mistakes |
| Lives in present | Lives in past or future |
| Is free from compulsions | Is compulsive and obsessive |

*Continued on next page.*

| | |
|---|---|
| Is not moved or stopped by fear | Is caught in fear |
| Can relate, make, and keep commitments | Is unable to commit because of fears |
| Is self-motivated | Is driven by outside forces |
| Has lively energy with serenity | Has nervous energy with anxiety |

Source: Adapted from Richo, D. (1999). *Shadow Dance*. Boston: Shambhala, p. 24.

### 2. Learning to Let Go

*Description:* The purpose is to illustrate the changes in thinking and behaving when we shift the ego from negative influence to positive.

*Instructions:* Ask participants to listen carefully to the tone as the words on the left column are read followed by the counterpart on the right column. After the columns are read, ask them how they felt and their thoughts during the exercise.

| As I let go of having to... | I become more able to... |
|---|---|
| Get my way | Cooperate with others |
| Insist my misdeeds be overlooked | Apologize and make amends |
| Be noticed and appreciated by everyone | Ask for, give, and receive appreciation |
| Insist I am not wrong | Be open to feedback |
| Feel devastated if I lose face | Admit an error |
| Make demands on others | Ask for what I want and need |
| Win, be loved, be respected | Ask for rightful credit and let go |
| Have to get back at others | Have a sense of justice, no need to punish |

Source: Adapted from Richo, D. (1999). *Shadow Dance*. Boston: Shambhala, p. 51.

## Personal Development Suggestions

### 1. Becoming Aware of the Dark Side

*Description:* The purpose of this exercise is to make you aware of the dark side of the ego.

*Instructions:* It is important to recognize when our dark side is emerging. We may be only subconsciously aware of our dark side, but there are signals that help us identify it. The goal is to identify these signals. Are you: Extremely driven to succeed? Constantly seeking approval? Perfectionist? Micromanager and controlling? Greedy? Jealous? Overly competitive? When you experience these behaviors, it is time to examine yourself and your motives because you are probably having a negative impact on others at work and at home.

### 2. The Flip Side of Success

*Description:* This exercise makes you realize that traits of success can also have a shadow side.

*Instructions:* Examine the success traits below and their flip sides. The purpose of the exercise is to bring awareness to both sides of the trait. When we are aware, we are able to control the dark side from dominating our behaviors. Do you see where success traits are positive and negative? When we are aware of both sides, we are better able to control the ego and not let the ego win.

| Confidence | Sense of infallibility |
|------------|------------------------|
| Alertness | Narrow focus |
| Control | Inflexibility |
| Charm | Manipulation |
| Commitment | Blind faith |

*Continued on next page.*

| Perseverance | Resistance to change |
|---|---|
| Dedication | Workaholism |

Source: Adapted from O'Neil, J. (1993).
*The Paradox of Success*. New York: G.P. Putnam's Sons.

## Readings

So much of leadership development is focused on skills and styles. Yet, understanding ego development is critical for success. Keeping the ego in balance requires leaders to be cognizant of what makes good leaders go bad. Pella Corporation in Pella, Iowa consistently makes *Fortune's* Best 100 Companies to Work list. They require all managers to read *The Servant* (1998) by James Hunter. In fact, the company brings in Hunter to lead workshops based on the book and "not letting the ego win."

In addition to the books cited in this chapter, I recommend *Shadow Dance: Liberating the Power & Creativity of Your Dark Side* (1999) by David Richo, and *Bad Leadership: What It Is, How It Happens, and Why It Matters* (2004) by Barbara Kellerman. A few other resources include books by Peter Frost: *Toxic Emotions at Work: How Compassionate Managers Handle Pain and Conflict* (2003) and *Toxic Emotions at Work: And What You Can Do About Them* (2007).

John O'Neil's book *The Paradox of Success* (1993) was ahead of its time. The book is just as relevant—if not more so—now as when it was written.

## What's Next

The next chapter explains how great leaders connect with empathy and compassion. These behaviors are often considered soft skills, but the consistent practice of these skills is anything but soft. This chapter explains why it is essential for leaders to understand some basic concepts of loss, death, and grief in order to have empathy and compassion for life's many transitions—including loss of jobs, position, power, and purpose at work and at home.

# Chapter 4

# Leaders Connect With Empathy and Compassion

*Our world cries out for great leaders with great wisdom, and we need*
*them now more than ever as so much hangs in the balance. These great*
*leaders care not for themselves, but for the whole of humanity and their*
*compassion and empathy is for the greatest good for the greatest number.*

—Judi Neal

*Empathy and compassion are two attributes that I see as among those that*
*are essential for all who are committed to lives spent in service to helping*
*the organization and all who work within, reach their highest potential.*

—Darlyne Bailey

The "Great Recession" of 2008 caused the loss of millions of jobs, shuttered hundreds of businesses and companies, and nearly collapsed the banking system. What is often overlooked in the recitation of economic facts and data is the human cost associated with economically hard times. When companies and industries disappear—and the jobs, relationships, and familiar ways of life with them—our human psyche naturally drives us to grieve for these losses even if we don't admit it. Hidden grief costs U.S. companies about $75.1 billion annually.

Based on several decades of survey data collected from more than 25,000 people who participated in the Grief Recovery© workshops, the consequences of grief include financial losses and difficulty in concentration that can result in errors in judgment, injuries, and accidents; unfortunately, the effects of grief can be misunderstood by others (Hazen, 2008, 78). Few, if any, business and MBA programs require courses on loss, death, and grief as part of their curriculum. Interestingly, the need for this understanding was noted many times during my interviews with leadership gurus and sages.

Richard Boyatzis, co-author of *Resonant Leadership* (2005), defines a resonant leader as one who demonstrates hope, compassion, and mindfulness. I asked him how it is possible to be a resonant leader in times of downsizing and budget cuts. Boyatzis had this response:

> *"Most people in management and leadership positions are not adding value—in good times and bad. During these economic times, it is becoming more evident how dysfunctional many leaders are. The only way to get out of economic disasters is to innovate and that requires full brain functioning. So the use of hope, mindfulness, and compassion become even more important if people are to work their way out of this mess.*
>
> *"But resonant leaders are always swimming against the current of what most people in leadership and management actually do. That is why it is so important to teach people the importance of becoming resonant leaders."*

My research revealed that one of the ways to help people connect with empathy and compassion is to embrace mortality. "The truth is, once you learn how to die, you learn how to live" (Albom, 1997, 82).

## Understanding Death to Understand Life

It's easy to understand why many high-energy, "master of the world" leaders don't give much thought to grief and loss. It's certainly not in their daily experience, their leadership training and development, or their leadership DNA. Yet, a number of these future and winning-focused leaders have been given a dose of life and death reality as a result of a near-death experience (NDE).

In 2009, management consultant Grant Thornton surveyed 250 CEOs of companies with revenues of $50 million or more. Twenty-two percent said they have had an experience when they believed they would die; and of those, 61 percent said it changed their long-term perspective on life or career. Forty-one percent said it made them more compassionate leaders; and 16 percent said it made them more ambitious. They describe how having a NDE helps them focus their priorities and lead a more balanced life (Jones, 2009). Even songwriter Tim McGraw reminds us in his song "Live Like You Were Dying" (on the album with the same title): "Someday I hope you get the chance to live like you were dying."

The late Steve Jobs, the iconic CEO of Apple Computer and one of the founders of Pixar Animation Studios, reported his own life-changing NDE during his 2005 commencement speech at Stanford University; a speech, by the way, that has received almost 17 million hits on YouTube, and the number continues to rise after almost a decade. One of the most cited sections of Job's speech is what he had to say on the subject of death (2005, 31-32):

*"Death is very likely the single best invention of Life. It is Life's change agent ... No one wants to die. Even people who want to go to heaven don't want to die to get there. And yet death is the destination we all share. No one has ever escaped it. And that is as it should be. Your time is limited so don't waste it living someone else's life. Don't let the noise of others' opinions drown out your own inner voice; and most important, have the courage to follow your heart and intuition."*

## Developing Compassion and Empathy

How many leadership development programs emphasize developing compassion and empathy? These are not skills typically taught in MBA programs, but they should be, based on my research. These are critical skills since our society tends—as Jobs points out—to be in denial about death—even though it is inevitable. The implication for leaders is clear. If we don't understand our own grief and coping mechanisms to face these inevitable topics, it is hard to help others with their own grief and loss when the time comes.

Unfortunately, compassion and empathy are usually labeled as "soft skills" under the category of interpersonal skills; therefore, they're not given the attention warranted. Still, leaders who understand and internalize these important skills use them to drive positive organizational results. A common theme among the sages was that "the soft stuff is the hard stuff." Joan Gallos, one of the sages, told me, "The fluff is the stuff!"

Since few leaders understand or have training to equip them to deal with loss and workplace grief or any of the other life events that manifest grief responses—serious illness, divorce, or the death of a spouse or partner—it is critical to learn how to transform grief into compassion and empathy. Interestingly, loss is even a component of many positive life events such as promotions and weddings. Associated with these positive events is often a grieving process for the way life used to be.

But in our culture, talking about loss and grief is usually taboo. We create arbitrary human resource policies that dictate how many days are allowed for major life losses such as the death of a family member or spouse. We somehow believe we can accurately quantify how long grief should last. It is time for that to change, because work is the place where a majority of our lives is spent. Leaders and the workplaces they create must be able to understand grief in ways that show compassion, minimize pain, and provide a healing environment.

## Leader's Responsibility

Deborah Morris Coryell, author of *Good Grief: Healing Through the Shadow of Loss* (2007), told me "It is the responsibility of leaders to make sure people have the resources they need to deal with loss and grief." She urges leaders to face their fears and explore their belief systems about grief and loss. Coryell said what leaders say to someone experiencing grief and how they say it is a "leadership moment" and that the best way to understand grief is to "stand under it."

Coryell explained that this deep, empathetic understanding of grief and loss is only possible if you actively seek self-understanding. She offered an analogy to illustrate her point. If you want to understand how your car operates or how a bridge is built you have to get under it to see "what is holding it up." Likewise, she said we need to "get under" our own beliefs about death, grief, and loss and explore our own comfort zones and the origins of our own beliefs. "You can only do with someone else what you have done yourself," she told me.

Beyond this self-knowledge, leaders need to learn how to communicate with healing language that is authentic and reflects compassion. This includes making time for rituals and ceremonies that acknowledge the loss and allow someone to learn to live with the loss. And in the end, transform the loss into Coryell's vision of "good grief," that is, grief that "we go through and live with, rather than get over."

David Noer, author of *Healing the Wounds: Overcoming the Trauma of Layoffs and Revitalizing Downsized Organizations* (1993), also expressed how important it is for leaders to understand the stages of grief to help others cope with their losses. In his book, Noer relates a story entitled "Metaphor of the Surviving Children" that is so good it's worth reading out loud (as I have in my own workshops) to any level of leaders in helping them understand how it might feel to be downsized out of an organization or to be left remaining as a "survivor." See the sidebar for the story.

## Metaphor of the Surviving Children

Imagine a family: a father, a mother, and four children. The family has been together for a long time, living in a loving, nurturing, trusting environment. The parents take care of the children, who reciprocate by being good.

Every morning the family sits down to breakfast together, a ritual that functions as a bonding experience, somewhat akin to an organizational staff meeting. One morning, the children sense that something is wrong. The parents exchange furtive glances, appear nervous, and after a painful silence, the mother speaks. "Father and I have reviewed the family budget," she says, looking down at her plate, avoiding eye contact, "and we just don't have enough money to make ends meet!" She forces herself to look around the table and continues, "As much as we would like to, we just can't afford to feed and clothe all four of you." After another silence she points a finger. "You two must go!"

"It's nothing personal," explains the father as he passes out a sheet of paper to each of the children. "As you can see by the numbers in front of you, it's simply an economic decision—we really have no choice." He continues, forcing a smile, "We have arranged for your aunt and uncle to help you get settled, to aid in your transition."

The next morning, the two remaining children are greeted by a table on which only four places have been set. Two chairs have been removed. All physical evidence of the other two children has vanished. The emotional evidence is suppressed and ignored. No one talks about the two who have disappeared. The parents emphasize to the two remaining children, the survivors, that they should be grateful, "since, after all, you've been allowed to remain in the family." To show their gratitude, the remaining children will be expected to work harder on the family chores. The father explains that "The workload remains the same even though there are two less of you." The mother reassures them that "This will make us a closer family!"

"Eat your breakfast, children," entreats the father. "After all, food costs money!"

Source: Noer, D. (1993). *Healing the Wounds: Overcoming the Trauma of Layoffs and Revitalizing Downsized Organizations.* San Francisco: Jossey-Bass Inc.

When Noer uses his Metaphor of the Surviving Children exercise, he found common themes in the responses. You might follow a similar line of questioning as Noer does below with the leaders in your own instructional programs.

1.  What were the children who left feeling? Most managers say, "anger," "hurt," "fear," "guilt," and "sadness."

2.  What were the children who remained feeling? Most managers conclude that the children who remain have the same feelings as those who left. Managers also report that the remaining children experience these feelings with more intensity than those who left.

3.  What were the parents feeling? Although the managers sometimes struggle with this question, most of them discover that the parents feel the same emotions as the surviving children.

4.  How different are these feelings from those of survivors in your organization? After honest reflection, many managers admit that there are striking and alarming similarities.

5.  How productive is a work force with these survivor feelings? Most managers conclude that such feelings are indeed a barrier to productivity. Some groups move into discussions about effects of survivor feelings on the quality of work life and share personal reflections.

This metaphor is a powerful way to personally feel the difficult choices being made in organizations and to understand why the metaphor of "family" is not as valued among employees (especially for the under-30 generation).

## Shifting From "Doing" to "Doing While Being"

Another way to help leaders connect with empathy and compassion involves writing one's own eulogy. The focus of most obituaries is on what the person has done or accomplished (doing). In contrast, the emphasis in eulogies is on who the person was as a person (being). Even though the tone and format of many obituaries are changing to sound more as eulogies, it is powerful to think about what you would want said at your funeral.

One of my PhD program professors thrived on teaching by the command and control model. He wanted us to be scared of him and fear his difficult exams. When he died, the family tightly controlled who could eulogize the former professor, fearing what would be said. As Frances Hesselbein, editor of the journal *Leader to Leader*, puts it, "Leadership is more about who we are rather than what we do" (Hesselbein, 2011, 213).

When doing the eulogy activity, participants know in advance that part of the assignment is to read their eulogies aloud. The format is completely open and it is an activity for participants of all ages. Note that this activity often brings up deep emotions, so don't be surprised if you have former football players in tears as they try to read what they have written. Still, this is great training for leaders willing to dig deep and do what is necessary to connect with those who look to them for strength, guidance, and compassion.

In 2009, I attended a presentation by André Delbecq, professor at Santa Clara University, at the Organizational Behavior Teaching Conference on "Exploring Personal and Organizational Responses to Suffering." Delbecq asked us to ponder this question that he referred to as the "litmus test" of the compassionate culture: "What would your organization do if you experienced a time of great difficulty?" Based on his research, he said that the typical organizational responses are either:

- Silence—They don't talk openly about it.

- Brief comments—"So are you OK?"

- Expect you to show up and "get over it."

Delbecq said these responses are because people in organizations don't know how to express feelings and compassion. Support requires a proactive response. People needing support are usually embarrassed by the difficulties, unaware of their rights and resources, and therefore carry the burden by themselves. Delbecq shared how senior leaders at Santa Clara University formed "strike teams" trained in appropriate responses to difficult or traumatic situations. Those on the "team" (faculty, administrators, and staff members) are taught to act with competence, consciousness, and compassion. What is interesting is that the university has found that paying attention to the "soft side" has made a big difference in creating a culture where people want to work.

## Understanding Transitions

While it sounds trite, it's true that "the only constant is change"—and change is accelerating daily. With change comes transition and with transition comes loss and uncertainty. Moving through life—both personally and professionally—is similar to swinging through a series of trapeze bars. It is scary to "let go" of what we have and are familiar with if we don't trust completely where we are going.

Numerous books and articles have been written on how leaders should "manage change," yet these resources often neglect to address leaders' need to understand the emotional dynamics of transitions so that they can help themselves and coach others through the process.

William Bridges, an authority on transitions, author of *The Way of Transition* (2001), and developer of a transition framework used by leaders in organizations and communities, told me that transition is the state that change creates and that "change is external (the different policy, practice, or structure that the leader is trying to bring about), while transition is an internal and psychological reorientation that people have to go through before the change can work."

Bridges continued by noting that moving through transitions leaves a person with wisdom.

> "Now we are aging young people without much wisdom. We are pushed from our past instead of cherishing it and learning from it. The implications for management are that many leaders are aging youthfully, but they are living out of their natural life phases. We have 60-year-old CEOs working 60 hours a week and they are not supposed to do that at that age. Therefore, we don't create the kind of environments that people need. The problems with leadership are the problems with maturing, developing, and growing. There is a pathological problem with adult development and this makes organizations toxic to the people in them."

The comments by Bridges connect with a strong theme that emerged during my interviews with leadership sages—adult development that includes the development of this "wisdom" should be part of leadership development programs.

I also interviewed Barbara Beizer, a transition coach and organizational development consultant. Beizer has been using Bridge's work for many years in leadership and organizational development in both the private and public sectors. She also maintains that many change initiatives are not sustainable because leaders do not understand the importance of transition.

Contrary to what we typically think, we don't resist change (external event). We resist the process of transition (the inner and emotional aspects involved with change). We resist letting go of the way it was or the way we thought it was. We resist taking on a new identity or embracing the new situation. In the Bridges framework, transition is made up of three stages:

1. **Endings:** often result in sadness, anger, or remorse. We start with endings because we don't begin something without ending something. We can't move ahead (as people and as organizations) without leaving something else behind. Something is being lost and we need to learn to let go. We need to realize that people grieve for these endings—for what was lost.

2. **The Neutral Zone:** results in fear and confusion. It is not so much that we are afraid of change or so in love with the old ways, but it's that place in between that we fear. This is when we are being caught between trapezes—dangling in the neutral zone.

3. **New Beginnings:** a mix of confidence over what has been gained and anxiety about what has been lost and worrying about slipping back into old habits.

Interestingly, we don't mind endings or new beginnings as much as we dread the neutral zone. That is why we go from one bad job to another, one bad relationship to another. We don't take the time in the neutral zone to process, reflect, and learn about why it ended or why the change took place.

When we don't understand the transition process, so many change initiatives fail or are poorly executed. This results in low productivity and higher costs as a result of an apathetic, disengaged, and emotionally drained workforce.

When leaders understand the issues involved in transition they make the resources and support needed available. It is critically important for the workforce to understand why the change is taking place and that transition is not always linear or automatic or successful. Everyone moves back and forth between feelings associated with endings and the neutral zone. Support, understanding, and patience must always be part of the process in order for people to successfully make it through the transition.

Bridges summarized the need for understanding this way: "No leader can effectively lead change—which is what leadership is all about—without understanding and ultimately, experiencing—the transition process." It is when we understand these stages, and the transitions between stages, that we can proactively make personal decisions that positively affect the quality of our professional and personal lives.

## Overcoming Fears

Since fear is a universal experience, it is one of the strongest emotions of all and it manifests itself in ways that negatively affects attitudes, performance, and interactions. The fear of death is one of the strongest fears. "The fear of death is the shadow of life. To elude the facing of death, the ego uses ambition, greed, procreation, acclaim, attempts to stave off aging, and many other desperate avoidances" (Richo, 1999, 39). Fear is the main reason many good leaders fail and workplaces become toxic.

And fear can be the glue that holds toxicity in organizations. Other ways it reveals itself can be in the form of bullying and blaming, sexual harassment, focus on scarcity, pain and suffering, dysfunction, and paralysis (Bailey et al., 2008). When a culture of fear is present, it affects levels of creativity, curiosity, eagerness to question, and compassion. It can turn "innocence into cynicism, curiosity into arrogance, and compassion into callousness" (Heifetz and Linksy, 2002, 226).

Richard Leider, one of the top executive coaches in the country, told me that he discovered through his research that people have four main fears:

- living a meaningless life
- being alone and not feeling connected
- being lost with no sense of community
- not having a purpose.

In 2009, I had the opportunity to attend a workshop at the Omega Institute with Pema Chodran, a Buddhist nun and one of the foremost students of Chogyam Trungpa, the renowned meditation master. She told the group of 500 that our biggest obstacle to compassion and kindness is the fear of feeling where we are in our lives. We fear unwanted and uncomfortable emotions. Chodran emphasized that the point is not to get rid of the anger and hurt, but to make "friends" with fear. When we do that, we free ourselves from fear.

Chodran pointed out that we cling to the ego, enclosing the self. And this becomes the root cause of suffering. Our natural tendency is to rid ourselves of "them" (boss, co-worker, or parent) and to think that it is someone else who is causing us to suffer. But instead of getting rid of someone or something, we should befriend it—which helps us to lose our fear of feeling whatever we are feeling. She warned us not to act on the fear or repress or deny it. She encouraged those attending her workshop to face it fully or to "get into it."

Chodran said there are two common exits to escape our fears: 1) acting, speaking, obsessing or 2) repressing, denying, and suppressing. But when we counterintuitively open to the fear and turn toward it—"lean into feeling the fear"—we can be one with the feeling and not let the fear drive our actions. Parker Palmer shared a story in his book *Let Your Life Speak* (2000) that illustrates "leaning into our fears." See the sidebar for the story.

# Leaning Into Fear

In my early forties, I decided to go on the program called Outward Bound. I was on the edge of my first depression, a fact I knew only dimly at the time, and I thought Outward Bound might be a place to shake up my life and learn some things I needed to know.

I chose the week-long course at Hurricane Island, off the coast of Maine ...Though it was a week of great teaching, deep community, and genuine growth, it was also a week of fear and loathing. In the middle of that week, I faced the challenge I feared most. One of our instructors backed me up to the edge of a cliff 100 feet above solid ground. He tied a very thin rope to my waist—a rope that looked ill-kempt to me and seemed to be starting to unravel—and told me to start "rappelling" down that cliff.

"Just go!" the instructor explained, in typical Outward Bound fashion.

So I went—and immediately slammed into a ledge, some four feet down from the edge of the cliff, with bone-jarring, brain-jarring force.

The instructor looked down at me: "I don't think you've quite got it."

"Right," said I, being in no position to disagree. "So what am I supposed to do?"

"The only way to do this," he said, "is to lean back as far as you can. You have to get your body at a right angle to the cliff so that your weight will be on your feet. It's counterintuitive, but it's the only way that works."

I knew that he was wrong, of course. I knew that the trick was to hug the mountain, to stay as close to the rock face as I could. So I tried it again, my way—and slammed into the next ledge, another four feet down.

"You still don't have it," the instructor said helpfully.

"OK," I said, "Tell me again what I am supposed to do."

"Lean way back," he said, "and take the next step."

The next step was a very big one, but I took it—and, wonder of wonders, it worked. I leaned back into empty space, eyes fixed on the heavens in prayer, made tiny, tiny moves with my feet, and started descending down the rock face, gaining confidence with every step...

I lowered my eyes and saw that I was approaching a deep hole in the face of the rock... The second instructor let me hang there, trembling, in silence, for what seemed like a very long time... then said, "It's time that you learned the Outward Bound motto."... She shouted 10 words I hope never to forget, words whose impact and meaning I can still feel:

"If you can't get out of it, get into it!"

There was no way out of my dilemma except to get into it... There is no way out of one's inner life so one had better get into it. On the inward and downward spiritual journey, the only way out is in and through.

Source: Palmer, P. (2000). *Let Your Life Speak*. San Francisco: Jossey-Bass Inc.

---

The country band Little Big Town has a song that really captures this "lean into fear" theme. The song is titled "Lean Into It" on their album *The Reason Why* and this is the chorus:

"There's a strong wind blowing
I push on—it pushes back
It's a hard time
But I know I'll get through it
Just gotta lean into it
Just gotta lean into it"

## Power of Rituals

Rituals can be another way of letting go of fears and moving through life transitions. A ritual is defined as "a rite, a ceremony, a series of symbolic acts focused toward fulfilling a particular intention … Rituals are an integral part of nature and our daily lives" (Beck and Metrick, 1990, 5). Rituals can be formal and elaborate, such as weddings, graduations, and funerals. They can also be more informal, but still infused with meaning. The ability to participate in ritual is important for personal growth, can provide cohesion of a group, and can reflect institutional memory.

In workshops and courses, I often read to participants a passage from the children's book *The Little Prince* (1943) by de Saint-Exupery to illustrate the purpose and value of rituals (see sidebar). While we can be connected 24 hours a day, seven days a week through technology, many people feel disconnected from one another. People have thousands of "friends" on Facebook, yet they don't have a handful of people they trust. Building a sense of community is explored in more detail in chapter 6. As social isolation has become more common and families are spread across the country, traditions and rituals have diminished. This makes the value of creating them in the workplace even more important.

# Fox and the Little Prince

*Note: This is a short excerpt from the full passage and includes a significant conversation about the meaning of the word "tame," something the fox says he is not.*

The fox fell silent and stared at the little prince for a long while. "Please... tame me!" he said.

"I'd like to," the little prince replied, "but I haven't much time. I have friends to find and so many things to learn."

"The only things you learn are the things you tame," said the fox. "People haven't time to learn anything. They buy things ready-made in stores. But since there are no stores where you can buy friends, people no longer have friends. If you want a friend, tame me!"

"What do I have to do?" asked the little prince.

"You have to be very patient," the fox answered. "First you'll sit down a little ways away from me, over there, in the grass. I'll watch you out of the corner of my eye, and you won't say anything. Language is the source of misunderstandings. But day by day, you'll be able to sit a little closer..."

The next day the little prince returned.

"It would have been better to return at the same time," the fox said. "For instance, if you come at four in the afternoon, I'll begin to be happy by three. The closer it gets to four, the happier I'll feel. By four I'll be all excited and worried; I'll discover what it costs to be happy! But if you come any old time, I'll never know when I should prepare my heart... There must be rites."

"What is a rite?" asked the little prince.

"That's another thing that's been too often neglected," said the fox. "It's the fact that one day is different from the other days, one hour from the other hours. My hunters, for example, have a rite. They dance with the village girls on Thursdays. So Thursday's a wonderful day; I can take a stroll all the way to the vineyards. If the hunters danced whenever they chose, the days would all be just alike, and I'd have no holiday at all."

Source: de Saint-Exupery, A. (1943). *The Little Prince*. Orlando: Harcourt, Inc., pp. 56-61.

Jim Autry, a pioneer in the "spirit at work" movement, wrote a poem for his groundbreaking book *Love and Profit: The Art of Caring Leadership* (1991) that communicates clearly why leaders should be aware of their own feelings and the feelings of others. I often read this poem aloud in classes and workshops. As I do, it is clear that the concepts resonate with the participants:

*What Personnel Handbooks Never Tell You*
*They leave a lot out of the personnel handbooks.*
*Dying for instance.*
*You can find funeral leave*
*but you can't find dying.*
*You can't find what to do*
*when a guy you've worked with since you both*
*were pups*
*looks you in the eye*
*and says something about hope and chemotherapy.*

*No phrases,*
*no triplicate forms,*
*no rating systems.*
*Seminars won't do it*
*and it's too late for a new policy on sabbaticals.*

*They don't tell you about eye contact*
*and how easily it slips away*
*when a woman who lost a breast*
*says, "they didn't get it all."*
*You can find essays on motivation*
*but the business schools*
*don't teach what the good manager says*
*to keep people taking up the slack*
*while someone steals a little more time*
*at the hospital.*
*There's no help from those tapes*
*you pop in the player*
*while you drive or jog.*
*They'd never get the voice right.*

*And this poem won't help either.*
*You just have to figure it out for yourself,*
*and don't ever expect to do it well.*

Source: *Love and Profit* by James A. Autry. Copyright© 1991 by James A. Autry.
Reprinted by permission of Harper Collins Publishers.

## Workshop Suggestions

1. **Write Your Own Eulogy**

   *Description:* This exercise guides your participants through the process of writing their eulogy for their funeral. When completed, participants are asked to read their composition out loud to everyone in the group.

   *Instructions:* What would you want people to say about you at your funeral? This can be written in first or third person. It also helps to talk with people who know you well to get their perspective. But it is important to think about how you want to be remembered.

2. **What's on Your Bucket List?**

   *Description:* This exercise makes people focus on what matters most when the end of life is in sight.

   *Instructions:* What things would you like to do or experience before you die?

   Make a list of the things you would like to do or experience before you die. Review the list. Find ways of making time to do or experience some of these things now. In reality, now is the only time we have. When will you have more time than now?

3. **Scripting Your Last Moments on Earth**

   *Description:* This exercise increases our familiarity with death as we script our last moments either as a journaling exercise or guided meditation.

   *Instructions:* Ask the following questions and have participants imagine and envision the answers. After asking the question, ask them: What did you learn from this experience?

- What music or sounds would you like to hear as you are dying?

- What poems, prayers, or sacred texts would you like recited?

- What would you like to taste?

- What scents would you like to smell?

- What objects would you like to have near you to touch and appreciate?

- What would you like your surroundings to look like?

- Whom would you like to be present?

- Whom would you definitely not invite to celebrate your departure from Earth?

- What would you like to say to those who have assembled around you? And what would you have them say to you?

- Is there anything else you might like in our final moments?

- What would you like to have done with your body?

- Who would you like to care for your body? And in what manner?

These steps help us to visualize, taste, smell, touch, and hear what we imagine to be our final moments on earth. Imagining these moments helps us become more comfortable in embracing our own mortality.

## 4. Create Rituals and Ceremonies

*Description:* This is an exercise to demonstrate the value of ritual. The kind of ceremony or ritual you create is not as important as how you conduct it.

*Instructions:* There are numerous ways to create a ritual or to conduct a ceremony. The focus should be on creating a spirit of intention, presence, and gratitude. Meaningful activities provide lasting memories that help us to let go in order to move on with our lives and to help others to do the same. Berta Parrish, in her book *Wise Woman's Way: A Guide to Growing Older* (1997), provides several suggestions:

- A lighted candle is passed around remembering or honoring the event.

- Build an altar of remembrance, as is done during the Mexican cultural celebration, Day of the Dead.

- Read "a letter to the world" that forgives and blesses the people and events in your life.

- Create rituals that involve sharing food, giving gifts, and writing scripts to be read aloud.

**5.  The Little Prince**

*Description:* This exercise involves reading a passage from a book to illustrate ritual.

*Instructions:* Read a passage (pages 56-61) from *The Little Prince.* Use it to illustrate the value of ritual. After reading the passage, ask people the following questions:

- Name some rituals or celebrations in your life.

- What if we celebrated birthdays on just any day? What if we did not celebrate weddings, graduations, or funerals? What is their value?

- What rituals or traditions do you have in your family?

- What purpose do they serve? What if we eliminated them?

## Personal Development Suggestions

**1.  Reflection Is Powerful**

*Description:* The purpose of this exercise is to learn from reflecting on one's life experience.

*Instructions:* Reflect on major life transitions you've experienced and jot notes about what they were, your experience of the in-between, past lessons learned that you gathered to assist you with the new, and the opportunities you opened to once on the other side.

## 2. Hospice Volunteer Training

*Description:* The purpose of this exercise is to be intentional about learning more about death, loss, and grief.

*Instructions:* One way to become comfortable with death, dying, and grieving is to be trained as a Hospice volunteer. Contact one of your local Hospice organizations and register for their volunteer training. Ideally, volunteering to spend time with people who are experiencing the death process helps us to become more comfortable with the idea of our own death. The training is excellent for the purpose of personal development and growth, regardless of whether you become an active volunteer or not. The training will help you become a better person and friend to those who need your support both in the workplace and outside of work.

## 3. Being Alive

*Description:* The purpose of this exercise is to focus on what it means to be fully alive with empathy and compassion.

*Instructions:* Presbyterian author Frederick Buechner suggests we think about death not as the cessation of bodily function, but ultimately as about life. In his book *Wishful Thinking: A Theological ABC* (1973), he asks a series of questions to get us to think about what it means to be fully alive. Buechner suggests we ask ourselves the following questions:

- Have you wept at anything during the past year?
- Has your heart beaten faster at the sight of young beauty?

- Have you thought seriously about the fact that someday you are going to die?

- More often than not, do you really listen when people are speaking to you instead of just waiting for your turn to speak?

- Is there anybody you know in whose place, if one of you had to suffer great pain, you would volunteer yourself?

And he concludes, "If your answer to all or most of these questions is no, then chances are that you are dead."

- To feel enough sorrow or pain or even joy that it causes weeping. This is to be fully alive.

- To notice beauty, whether in another person or a moment or this world, and feel the heart skip a beat, is to be alive.

- To contemplate one's death and that time is limited; and to try and work on more patience, forgiveness, and love is to be alive.

- To listen… to God… to others… is to be alive.

- To care enough about others or a cause or even a bedraggled institution like the church, and to know that it is worth sacrificing self and suffering pain for its gain, is to be alive.

## Readings

A favorite book on the topics in this chapter includes the classic *Tuesdays With Morrie* (Albom, 1997). This is a quick nonfiction book that beautifully integrates the concepts of sage-ing: death, fear, compassion, aging, forgiveness, and legacy. This book was also made into a TV movie that was Jack Lemmon's last starring role, for which he won an Emmy award. *Good Grief: Healing Through the Shadow of Loss* (2007) by Deborah Morris Coryell is an excellent book on grief. In the 10th anniversary edition a 60-minute CD is included, which you can listen to for reinforcement.

William Bridges is recognized as one of the authorities on life's transitions. I particularly value his book *The Way of Transition: Embracing Life's Most Difficult Moments* (2001). *The Evolving Self: A Psychology for the Third Millennium* (1994) by Mihaly Csikszentmihalyi is an excellent book for understanding how we continue to evolve. For workshops, I recommend *Becoming a Resonant Leader: Develop Your Emotional Intelligence, Renew Your Relationships, and Sustain Your Effectiveness* (2008) by Annie McKee, Richard Boyatzis, and Frances Johnston.

## What's Next?

In the next chapter, we explore how admitting mistakes fearlessly is a characteristic of effective leaders, and it includes self-forgiveness and the forgiveness of others. Admitting mistakes allows others to trust us. We trust others more easily as well. We realize that vulnerability can be a strength. The winner in this trust dance is the organization and all those who work in a healthy, open environment.

# Chapter 5

# Leaders Admit
# Mistakes Fearlessly

*Leaders need to be people of integrity who are willing to admit mistakes,*
*show that they care, and be vulnerable and honest.*
—Ray Anderson
*When we are open to being vulnerable, we know we are fully alive.*
—Zalman Schachter-Shalomi

I attended a leadership development workshop in Boston facilitated by Peter Senge. On the second day, he walked into the classroom clearly in a circumspect mood. He took a few minutes to compose himself before sharing the disturbing news that one of his teenage son's best friends had been killed in a car accident the previous night. He went on to share that he considered the young man as another son and that the incident was another reminder of what matters most in life.

Senge's willingness to share his emotions and vulnerability made the class feel connected to his pain, and in the end, it was a sign of his strength and authenticity as a leader. Similar to the matryoshka dolls described in chapter 2, human beings consist of layers. It is hard to peel back the layers to learn who we are and what is important to us. We learn early in life to put up our guard, to not show all of our cards, to wear masks, to play the game, to "fake it until we make it." We also learn to avoid mistakes and to not admit we've made mistakes at all costs. Maybe that's why so many in leadership roles assume they are somehow vulnerable if they don't have the answer to every question.

John Hope Bryan, in *Love Leadership: The New Way to Lead in a Fear-Based World*, uses the phrase "vulnerability is power." Interestingly, "the paradox is that by acknowledging your vulnerabilities, you retain the power because others are unable to take advantage of you when you try to cover up your shortcomings and fears…. You empower others to become more authentic by acknowledging their vulnerabilities" (Synder, 2013, xii).

In the larger culture in which we live, the trend seems to seek out "hero leaders" who are charismatic and can be placed on a pedestal. These leaders may have a high-profile style, but the dark side may be that their sense of entitlement, difficulty accepting responsibility for mistakes, and addiction to perfection is a defensive reaction to unaddressed fear. And leaders who cannot face or admit to fear and vulnerability are incapable of demonstrating empathy and caring leadership. This is not to say that these leaders avoid making difficult choices when they must. It's part of the job. But leaders willing to share their own fears are the authentic leaders others want to follow.

Jim Autry, author of *Love and Profit* (1991), said it best when he told me: "Tough times are not the times to get tough. Even though times are tough, leaders still need to find good people, help them to be more productive, and assure them of their connection to the organization in order to accomplish goals together."

## Dare to Be Courageous and Humble

If you look up *humility* in the dictionary you'll find that it is defined as "modesty" or "lacking pretense" or "not believing that you are superior to others." Some dictionaries may include an ancillary definition of "having a lowly opinion of oneself" or "meekness."

Jim Collins, in his seminal work *Good to Great: Why Some Companies Make the Leap...and Others Don't* (2001), discovered that humility was a characteristic of the best leaders. These are the leaders who direct their egos away from themselves and toward the larger goal of leading their company to greatness. These leaders are a complex, paradoxical mix of intense professional will and extreme personal humility. They create superb results, but shun public adulation, and are never boastful.

Collins uses the metaphor of the "window and the mirror" to explain these top-level leaders' humility. They look out the "window" to give credit to others and they look in the "mirror" to place blame when things don't go as planned. This is how leaders demonstrate strength— through admitting mistakes and being willing to be vulnerable.

On one of my personal retreats to the New Melleray Abbey, I spoke to Father Jonah about humility. He told me that knowing that we came from the earth and that we are not God reminds us not to play the role of God. Father Jonah explained it this way:

> *"Humility plays a critical role in monastic life because we follow the Rule of St. Benedictine....The art of being human is when the human knows what matters most—that there is something greater than ourselves. When you know what matters most, then you can determine the value of experiences and situations you encounter. You can assess*

*how they help you reach what matters most. Does what I*
*want to do contribute or detract from what matters most?*
*What the heart is set on is something that endures and*
*doesn't go out of style, because it guides our actions and*
*behaviors and contributes to what matters most.... If*
*organizations are focused on what matters most, then they*
*unburden with what is unnecessary."*

Leaders face times when they must admit to not knowing the answers. Admitting this and seeking others' input requires humility, and it's an important milestone in a leader's development. In fact, I think one of the greatest strengths of a leader is to admit mistakes and ask for forgiveness if someone has been hurt unnecessarily. Most people can "let go" and move on if there has been an acknowledgment of some injustice—intended or unintended. When we don't understand this, an organization can become toxic to people who work within it.

## Leaning Into Fear

Likewise, it takes courage to embrace our life experiences and to learn from them. In fact, wisdom comes from processing our life experiences. As described in chapter 4, leaning into fear helps us become more empathetic and compassionate. It also enables us to become more authentic as we admit mistakes and are able to be vulnerable. André Delbecq teaches a course at Santa Clara University called "Spirituality for Business Leadership MBA." The students are challenged directly to face their fears through an exercise that asks participants to identify one of their greatest fears and to interact with someone who has had (or is having) that life experience.

For example, if the student feared death then he might arrange to interact with someone in a hospice facility. Or, if the student is fearful of entering a room full of strangers, she might actively seek out someone who has overcome this fear. The idea of the exercise is to understand a particular fear or anxiety, and to a develop compassion and empathy for others who share the same problem. Ideally, the exercise allows the students to release their fear and set themselves free.

Through economic position and role, leaders are often sought out as potential benefactors or contributors to those less fortunate. But as a benefactor, we may appear sympathetic and condescending. The purpose of this exercise is to be a companion by the side. The objective is being with, rather than doing for; listening to and learning from; and reflecting on the life experience in order to face our fears. This exercise, "Being With the Other," is included in the workshop section at the end of this chapter.

We talk about the value and wisdom in learning to "let go" to become empathetic and compassionate with others. It is when we face our fears that we learn to understand our emotions so that our emotions don't control us. When you know what pain is, then you can empathize with those in pain. People of all ages and life experiences find that the encounter helps them learn about themselves and therefore gain self-insight—awaken to one's self.

When we approach situations from a perspective of humility and willingness to learn from others, we forget about being perfect and we enjoy being in the moment. Demonstrating vulnerability also invites people to connect with one another and it allows others to see that we are just as human as they are.

Still, it takes courage to be vulnerable. The original definition of courage is from the Latin word *cor*, meaning "heart." And the original definition was to tell the story of who you are with your whole heart.

Maya Angelo said it best at a keynote I attended a few years ago: "Without courage, you can't practice any other virtue consistently: Be consistently fair, consistently just, consistently merciful, [and] consistently loving."

Likewise, Suku Radia, the CEO of a large bank, told me that leadership is a matter of having our hearts in the right place. "Is it not true that what we know really well, we 'know by heart'? When we take something seriously, do we not 'take it to heart?' When one does something abhorrent, do we not say, 'Where is your heart?' [Yet] when we are discouraged, we 'lose heart.' Conversely, when we find courage, we have 'found our hearts.' When we sense something in our entire being, we 'feel it in our hearts.' And when we have learned by heart, we act on what we know."

## Forgiveness

When I asked the sages how to best prepare leaders in these uncertain times, a strong theme in the responses was learning to forgive ourselves as a pathway to greater empathy and compassion. Without the example of forgiveness from the top, workplaces become toxic as grudges, resentment, anger, and bitterness trickle down and snuff out positive emotions in the workplace.

Pema Chodran, an ordained nun and Buddhist teacher, put it this way in a workshop I attended on "Loving to Oneself and Merciful to Others" at the Omega Institute in New York: "Moment by moment we have a choice—an opportunity to reinforce confusion and old habits or choose freedom." She noted that this freedom often involves forgiving ourselves and others.

Learning to forgive is good for both our mental and physical well-being, and our relationships. Since leadership is more about relationship than position, it is important to learn how to forgive to effectively move on in our lives and create healthy workplaces.

Dr. Fred Luskin, author of *Forgive for Good: A Proven Prescription for Health and Happiness* (2003), says forgiveness eases emotional distress, allows people to think more clearly, and helps end the vicious cycle of blame and a grievance story. According to Luskin, his studies reveal:

- People who are more forgiving report fewer health problems.
- Forgiveness leads to less stress.
- Forgiveness leads to fewer physical symptoms of stress.
- Failure to forgive may be more important than hostility as a risk factor for heart disease.
- People who blame other people for their troubles have higher incidences of illnesses such as cardiovascular disease and cancers.

But what is forgiveness?

- Forgiveness is for you and not the offender.
- Forgiveness is taking back your power.
- Forgiveness is taking responsibility for how you feel.
- Forgiveness is about your healing and not about the people who hurt you.
- Forgiveness is a trainable skill just like learning to throw a baseball.
- Forgiveness helps you get control over your feelings.
- Forgiveness is becoming a hero instead of a victim.
- Forgiveness is a choice.
- Everyone can learn to forgive.

In my leadership workshops and classes, I often cite how the Amish reacted to the horrific October 2006 slaying of five young schoolgirls in Pennsylvania as a powerful example of forgiveness. Newspapers, online posts, and the book *Amish Grace: How Forgiveness Transcended Tragedy* (2010) gave us a moving portrait of a community that understands the power of healing relationships.

According to a *New York Times* article published shortly after the tragedy, it is not unusual for the Amish to reach out to those who hurt them. "When an Amish dies in a car accident, the motorist is often invited to the funeral ... because such encounters help survivors heal," the article said. It was reported that an Amish neighbor wrapped his arms around the gunman, Carl Roberts IV, for an hour while expressing words of forgiveness (Dewan, 2006).

Leaders are human and humans make mistakes. Sincerely apologizing for mistakes made and forgiving others for their imperfections are powerful actions for leaders. We can learn a great deal about practicing compassion and forgiveness by observing the actions, behaviors, and words of the Amish. When such behavior is demonstrated, leaders cast more light than darkness in the workplace.

## Trust and Gratitude

Much discussion is taking place about the deficit of trust. While it builds over time, it can be fractured in an instant. In *The Speed of Trust: The One Thing That Changes Everything* (2006), Stephen Covey and Rebecca Merrill talk about organizations who in 360-degree feedback processes ask their employees directly: "Do you trust your boss?" These companies report that the answer to this one question is a better predictor of team and organizational performance than any other question they might ask. Based on his life experiences, Ray Rood told me that "we need more high touch and low tech. People will follow you through deep waters when trust exists. But this takes courage for leaders."

One theme that emerged among the sages was that to be trusted we must trust others. When we trust others, they tend to trust us. As one sage said, "You build trust by being trustworthy." Creating a culture of trust includes admitting mistakes and allowing others to admit mistakes too. Only then, can we learn from the mistakes being made.

In cultivating trust, it also helps to develop an attitude of gratitude. While it is easy to say "count your blessings," it is often difficult to do. When we focus on giving thanks, it is easier to think about what we have in abundance instead of being mired in an attitude based on competition and scarcity. For those in leadership roles, it is good to remember that others, including those you lead, want to be around leaders who express gratitude for both the large and small gifts in their lives.

That's why I cultivate in those who attend my courses and workshops an "attitude of gratitude." One assignment requires participants to write a personal note of gratitude (use paper—no emails) to someone who has made a difference in their lives. I usually distribute a postcard that says, "I am grateful" on the front. In the next workshop or class session, I ask participants to share how they felt when they wrote the note and share any response they received. Often the participants remark on how taking the extra time to personally write a note adds value and meaning to the exercise and to those receiving the notes.

I also incorporate gratitude journals into my courses and workshops. Research indicates that feelings of gratitude can have dramatic positive effects on individual and organizational performance (Whetton and Cameron, 2011). Those who keep gratitude journals feel better about their lives as a whole and have higher states of alertness, energy, and wellness.

Since developing an attitude of gratitude is a habit, actions and behaviors of gratefulness need to be practiced. Maintaining a gratitude journal helps us pay attention to our actions and the actions of others. Gratitude journals are explained in more detail in the Workshop Suggestions section. Developing this attitude is even more important earlier than later in our lives. It involves reframing how we view people, relationships, and situations. Being grateful helps us overcome our fears. Gratitude also helps us be more compassionate and empathetic while we forgive others and ourselves. When we are grateful, we live our best life.

## Workshop Suggestions

### 1. Repairing Relationships

*Description:* This exercise is to help reframe relationships in order to repair them.

*Instructions:* A powerful reframing exercise is called "A Testimonial Dinner to the Severe Teachers." This practice helps in forgiveness and creates more positive feelings by reframing the situation. You can use this exercise to heal hurtful situations of the past.

Divide a piece of paper into three columns. In the first column, make a list of the people who have wronged you; in the second column, describe the apparent injustice that was inflicted on you; and in the last column, explore how it has benefited you in unexpected ways. To each of the offending parties, say, "I understand now that you did me a great deal of good by your words and actions when you said \_\_\_\_\_ and did \_\_\_\_\_ for which I want to thank you. I understand now that it was difficult for you, and it was difficult for me, too. But now I forgive you and I am grateful for your contribution to my life" (Schachter-Shalomi and Miller, 1995, 118).

## 2. Gratitude Journal

*Description:* The purpose of this exercise is to keep an ongoing gratitude journal in a simple notebook.

*Instructions:* Document those things, people, or events for which you are grateful and give the reasons. The quality of the writing is not important, but it is getting your thoughts down about people and items for which you are thankful. You don't have to write in complete sentences and the writing does not have to flow. Use bullet points if that helps get the process moving. But complete the thought. For example: "The sun is bright today! When the sun is shining, I feel more positive than when it is cloudy." Cultivating and reinforcing an attitude of gratitude also helps in reframing situations and relationships.

## 3. Gratitude Letter

*Description:* This exercise is about having participants write a letter or note to someone to whom they feel a sense of gratitude.

*Instructions:* Write a handwritten letter and mail it or hand deliver it to the person. I recommend not using email because handwriting is more personal. If you are also keeping a gratitude journal, document in your journal how you felt during the process of writing the letter. While the content of the letter is personal, write in your journal about the response or reaction of the person receiving your note of appreciation and thanks.

## 4. Being With the "Other"

*Description:* This exercise is adapted from André Delbecq, who uses this exercise with CEOs and other top executives to achieve greater effectiveness in leading organizations. I adapted the exercise and have used it both in undergraduate and graduate leadership courses.

*Instructions:* The purpose of the field experience is to be with those who are marginalized in order to develop empathy and compassion. Organizational leaders, through socioeconomic position and role, are sometimes separated from the poor and suffering. This is not to imply that suffering doesn't touch all our families and friends through illness, aging, death, misfortune, and other trials. Yet, there are resources available to families of the business leaders that are often not available to others.

The purpose of this field experience is to be with those who are marginalized and therefore excluded from leadership roles and the socioeconomic status these roles grant. The focus is on:

- being with, rather than doing for
- listening to and learning from
- prayerfully or meditatively reflecting on the experience.

The challenge is to interact in an environment you might fear. If you fear death, have an encounter with the dying. If you fear being disabled, visit with those who are disabled. Choose an encounter with those presently unable to engage in active participation in our economic system. For example: HIV patients in later stages of their illness, chronically ill, the aged, the disabled, and so on.

This is an experience with a person, not with a category of people. Listen to the individual voice and pay attention to the life story. What have you learned from being with someone who has life experiences that you fear? What have you learned about yourself? What have you learned about compassion and empathy?

## Personal Development Suggestions

### 1. Practice Humility

*Description:* Participants are encouraged to build humility into their leadership practices and do so by example.

*Instructions:* Be intentional about giving credit to others (look out the window) and accepting blame (look in the mirror) when appropriate. Every time you share credit for successes with others (look in the mirror), you reinforce this behavior for others. Consider mentoring or coaching emerging leaders on this key attribute of leadership. Admit mistakes, be accountable, and take responsibility because others probably already know.

### 2. Understanding Regret

*Description:* This exercise helps us come to terms with the power of regret. The objective is to be able to live *with* regret without living *in* regret. Most people have regret for what they did and should not have done, and regret for what they did not do and should have done.

*Instructions:* Write a yes or no to the questions below. Then ask yourself, "How?" The questions are to stimulate introspection and the answers are not shared publicly. Could I have been a better...

- Mother or father?
- Wife or husband?
- Boss?
- Employee?
- Friend?
- Sibling?
- Neighbor?

Source: Adapted from Autry, J. (2012). *Choosing Gratitude.*
Macon, GA: Smyth & Helwys Publishing, Inc.

### 3. Regrets, Consequences, and Amends

*Description:* This exercise reminds us of the value of writing down regrets, consequences, and lessons learned from reflecting on mistakes made.

*Instructions:* Complete the following sentences: "I regret saying_____." "I regret doing_____." "I regret not saying_____." "I regret not doing_____." What did you feel as you were completing these sentences? Now write down the consequences you experienced or perceived reactions from these words or actions. After reflection, what should you have done? What should you have said? And the final question: Is there something you should do now to change or mitigate the consequences? Do you need to make amends or ask for forgiveness? "Making amends is a gift to yourself. Asking forgiveness is a gift to yourself" (Autry, 2012, 104-105).

### 4. Naikan

*Description:* This is a Buddhist meditation and exercise that helps us see the reciprocal quality of relationships.

*Instructions:* Ask yourself these three questions:

What have I received from _____?

What have I given to _____?

What troubles and difficulties have I caused?

Source: Adapted from Arrien, A. (2011). *Living in Gratitude: A Journal That Will Change Your Life*. Boulder, CO: Sounds True, Inc.

## Readings

The topics covered in this chapter sound easy, but are hard to practice. As Jim Autry says in his book *Choosing Gratitude: Learning to Love the Life You Have* (2012), "Gratitude does not come naturally. We have to learn it." Likewise, forgiveness is a complicated topic, but understanding how to forgive yourself and others is a powerful gift both at work and at home. And humility is essential for great leaders. I highly recommend these books: *Good to Great: Why Some Companies Make the Leap...and Others Don't* (2001) by Jim Collins, *Forgive for Good: A Proven Prescription for Health and Happiness* (2003) by Frederic Luskin, *Amish Grace: How Forgiveness Transcended Tragedy* (2010) by Donald Kraybill, Steven Nolt, and David Weaver-Zercher.

## What's Next?

Organizations are systems of interconnected parts similar to the communities in which we live. The best leaders are social architects working to build high-functioning organizations, but the work is not easy to finesse. Chapter 6 discusses this community concept and how managers and other leaders can use this connection with community in their organizations and in their own community where they live to lead more effectively.

# Chapter 6

## Leaders Embrace Community

*Without community, people lose their meaning,*
*purpose, usefulness—they develop fears.*
—Peter Block

*Do we consider organizations as well-oiled machines or of*
*living organisms consisting of interconnected people?*
—Meg Wheatley

Peter Senge's classic book *The Fifth Discipline* (1990) introduced the phrase *systems thinking* to the business practice lexicon as a way to remind us that decisions have ramifications across the organization. The concept that the most efficient organizations ensure their functional parts operate interdependently rather than independently is hard to dispute. Especially since "many organizations appear to be collection of people operating within their own domains, rather than a domain of people collectively operating" (Bailey, et al., 2008, 17).

Early in 2009, Tom Brokow said the following on MSNBC, which I paraphrase:

*We need to reset our economy instead of viewing it as
a cycle. Now there is a heightened sense of conscious
interconnectedness. People are realizing that we are all in
this together. We have to reset our expectations, create a new
kind of ethos, and focus on values—on what really matters.*

The best leaders work to establish functional and departmental connections, not only to share essential information within the companies they lead, but also to build a sense of trust and mutual respect for everyone in the organizational community. It is easy to characterize an organization as a "family" but often the decisions leaders make (either by choice or compelling circumstance) are destructive to notions of community. These decisions—layoffs, downsizing, and other traumatic events that happen in organizations—push a workforce to be distrustful, defensive, isolated, fearful, and unproductive. Great leaders minimize the impact of their decisions by simply engaging honestly with their organizational community. An often-told children's story illustrates this point well.

The story involves three soldiers who come to a town and ask for food. Unfortunately, the region is beset by famine so the peasants in the village hid what food they have and claim they have no food to share. Undaunted, the soldiers accept what the villagers say and set about to make stone soup instead. The soldiers gather up stones from around the village and place them in a big pot filled with water. As the fascinated villagers look on, the soldiers light a fire under the pot and then stand by watching as the water begins to boil.

Eventually, one of the soldiers mentions to the gathered crowd that the soup would be much better if only some carrots could be added. Soon, a villager shows up with an apron full of carrots. Then, another soldier points out how the soup's flavor would be improved with the addition of cabbage. Another villager leaves the gathered crowd and returns with that ingredient. Soon, the boiling pot is thick with beef, potatoes, barley, and milk. Slowly, the same thought occurs to each villager gathered around the steaming pot. Soon all the villagers are smiling at each other as they realize that their actions as a community created a pot of soup large enough to feed not only the hungry soldiers, but everyone else in the village.

This story from the classic book *Stone Soup* (1947) by Marcia Brown illustrates a point that nearly all the 100-plus sages I interviewed emphasized. That despite our natural self-preservation tendency to hoard during scarcity, we always discover that we have more than we think we have when we make an effort to connect and share. However, this sense of connection is easy to lose in the middle of downsizings or layoffs or other unavoidable organizational trauma.

The word *community* highlights its meaning of being one in unity. Effective leaders think of those in their organization or department or team as a family or group holding onto the same rope. When someone pulls on the rope, all people holding on are affected. It's a point that Peter Senge makes when he defines systems thinking as a "shift of mind—from seeing ourselves as separate from the world to connected to the world, from seeing problems as caused by someone or something 'out there' to seeing how our own actions create the problems we experience."

## Growing Isolation and Loneliness

According to Patrick Overton in *Rebuilding the Front Porch of America* (1997), we are losing our "front porch"—our gathering place. He describes how our culture is slowly "dis-integrating" as we lose "groundedness" and connection to core values that keep communities and even nations together. "We are untethered, disconnected from one another," causing some to feel isolated and alone. As a society, we are "drifting and confused—unsure of the roles and the rules—caught in the middle of a social and economic upheaval." The front-porch metaphor is in stark contrast to how we spend our lives today, focused on our smartphone screens or cut off from the world by "ear buds" that communicate a message of "Don't talk to me!"

Research has documented this social isolation. In a face-to-face study of 1,467 adults that mirrors a study done 20 years ago, one-fourth of all Americans report that they have nobody to talk to about "important matters." Another quarter reported they are just one person away from having nobody. But the most startling finding was that in only two decades, from 1985 to 2004, the number of people who have no one to talk to has doubled and the number of confidants has gone down from three to two (McPhearson, Smith-Lovin, and Brashears, 2006).

This is significant because "the closer and stronger our tie with someone, the broader the scope of their support for us and the likelihood that they will provide major help in a crisis." This is a strange finding given our ability to constantly communicate with each other. It seems we prefer our relationships online, separated by time and distance, over deep friendships in our own backyard.

"Socially connected people live longer, respond better to stress, have more robust immune systems, and do better at fighting a variety of specific illnesses," the authors point out. "These medical benefits derive directly from the social connection itself, not just from lifestyle improvement, such as better diet, more exercise, and better medical care." They agree with Robert Putnam, author of the classic *Bowling Alone: The Collapse and Revival of American Community* (2000) and co-author *of Better Together: Restoring the American Community* (2003), that feeling connected and part of a community is vitally important in many ways.

In his book, *The Pursuit of Loneliness: American Culture at the Breaking Point* (1976), Philip Slater made this point about being alone long before development of social networking and the Internet: "We seek a private house, a private means of transportation, a private garden, a private laundry, self-service stores, and do-it-yourself skills of every kind. An enormous technology seems to have set itself the task of making it unnecessary for one human being ever to ask anything of another in the course of going about his daily business. Even within the family, Americans are unique in their feeling that each member should have a separate room, and even a separate telephone, television, and car when economically possible. We seek more and more privacy, and feel more and more alienated and lonely when we get it" (p. 5).

Today's technology should be used as a tool, not as a replacement for human contact. Peter Block used this example to make this point. "Only 70 percent of an image in a mirror is reflected. Technology can't transmit the essence of a person and it can't replace the senses. We miss the nuances of people and who they are. It just can't substitute for relatedness. When we keep people apart, they are easier to control and that is not a good thing."

Peter Block also describes in *Community: The Structure of Belonging* (2008) that there is a strong need to create a structure of belonging because of the "isolated nature of our lives, our institutions, and our communities....Ironically, we talk today of how small our world has become, with the shrinking effect of globalization, instant sharing of information, quick technology, workplaces that operate around the globe. Yet, these do not necessarily create a sense of belonging." While they provide connection, diverse information, and a variety of opinions, "all of this does not create the connection from which we can become grounded and experience the sense of safety that arises from a place where we are emotionally, spiritually, and psychologically a member."

Given the independent mindset of most people, it is not surprising that teamwork and collaboration are challenging issues for organizations. It is also not surprising that people who don't know each other do not feel connected. This leads to the apprehension of trusting both leaders and co-workers. When people don't know each other well, the lack of trust makes it difficult to work together effectively.

But leaders who take these conditions to heart will work hard to overcome these roadblocks to community building by engaging leaders, listening more, and talking less. Many of the sages advocated practicing the simple principle of management by walking around (MBWA). The point is to get out of the office in order to get to know the employees better. As research has revealed, if most people have fewer people whom they trust and in whom they can confide, then maybe the most important actions and behaviors leaders can develop is to create the time and space to listen and be present; not give advice, answers, or feedback. Just listen in order to connect and build a sense of community. The simple fact is that leaders who honestly connect with their workforce are less controlling. And that's certainly a practice that suits the times.

## Building Community

Building a community requires a different kind of leader—one with the capacity to convene and engage citizens (employees) differently. The role decentralizes leadership and therefore takes the burden off leaders to be leaders. Instead, leaders become conveners. The most powerful form of leadership is to convene people around a possibility, not a problem. We change the culture by changing the conversation.

Peter Block told me, "We need to take off the table questions of style, behavior, walking the talk, articulating the vision, and enrolling behavior. We need to bring the leader back to earth. At the end of the day, the leader is not that important. Leaders tend to be more powerful in destroying something rather than creating and maintaining. Our current culture romanticizes leaders, but leadership should be replaced with citizenship. Employees should change the way they support one another. Employee relationships are where the action is and this is based on a sense of community. A stronger sense of community is a solution and answer to many of our problems."

Father Jonah, the guestmaster and one of the monks at New Melleray Abbey, explained community in this way:

> *"We need to have a personal story that we are living up to. Organizations help us live this story in community. A mission should be a shared story of the organization that is talked about one-on-one, in groups, and in large settings. The story can be shared orally and in writing, but it should be constantly referenced as a reminder to live the story and keep it alive. In the absence of this story, the void is filled by seeking personal gains rather than working for the common good. This is how we create a culture and why culture is so important. In times*

*of temptation or when we need support, we can turn to others*
*in the organization who are living the story."*

To illustrate the importance of connections and support groups, consider the examples of Alcoholics Anonymous and Weight Watchers. Success is usually attributed to the support of the group. It is so hard to fight the fight alone, but the power of the group manifested through the building of community made it possible. These groups, particularly AA, provide fellowship for life. Corporate America needs to take a lesson from these and other groups that convene around a support community.

We don't use the power of the group enough in corporate America. A sense of community is also the genius of Dale Carnegie. The group holds us accountable and we don't want to disappoint the group. The group requires transparency about our goals and commitments. It also provides a healing environment because of the support provided. Likewise, if we try to sabotage the process, everyone knows and the group can throw us out! The process has a way of eliminating or weeding people out by making them uncomfortable.

## The Power of Connection

Senator and former presidential candidate John McCain spent more than five years in captivity as a POW in North Vietnam. After he was released, he wrote an article for the May 14, 1973 issue of *U.S. News & World Report* in which he described how he managed to survive this captivity ordeal. He describes how he kept his mind busy and devised complex communication methods to connect to other solitary confinement prisoners. McCain provides a lesson about the power of connection and how critical it was for survival. See the sidebar for McCain's story.

# Communication Was Vital "for Survival"

As far as this business of solitary confinement goes—the most important thing for survival is communication with someone, even if it's only a wave or a wink, a tap on the wall, or to have a guy put his thumb up. It makes a difference....

The story of Ernie Brace illustrates how vital communication was to us. While I was in the prison we called "The Plantation" in October, 1968, there was a room behind me. I heard some noise in there so I started tapping on the wall.

For two weeks I got no answer, but finally, back came the two taps.... Then I said, "Put your ear to the wall." I finally got him up on the wall and by putting my cup against it, I could talk through it and make him hear me. I gave him the tap code and other information. He gave me his name—Ernie Brace....

It took me several days to get him back up on the wall again. When I finally did, all he could say was, "I'm Ernie Brace," and then he'd start sobbing. After about two days he was able to control his emotions, and within a week this guy was tapping and communicating and dropping notes, and from then on he did a truly outstanding job.

Source: May 14, 1973, *U.S. News & World Report*.

Yes, it is easy to be available for "work" 24 hours a day and seven days a week, but the point of McCain's story is that we have become prisoners to being connected. Leaders need to consider the creativity, innovation, and community cost of being virtually connected all the time. Sometimes disconnecting is just what is needed to connect.

## Ways to Build Community

So how do leaders disconnect in order to connect and build community? You'll find a number of techniques and other exercises in the Workshop Section at the end of this chapter. One favorite exercise is the "talking stick," so named because the person holding the "stick"—an actual stick or even a pencil or other object will do as well—has the "floor" and the ability to express what they are thinking or feeling. This exercise also requires participants with the "stick" to practice their listening skills—essential for finding common ground and for getting to know one another better and at a deeper level. The exercise is often associated with Native American culture and it encourages all participants to respect the opinions of others and withhold judgment.

Jim Collins often says in his presentations about leaders, "It is more important to be interested than interesting." What Collins means is that when we are "interesting," the focus is internal—on ourselves—and more self-centered. When you are interested, you ask questions and you're intentional about having them share more about themselves. Asking questions of others is a simple way to start building relationships. It indicates a desire to get to know them and it provides an opportunity for them to share their story.

## One-on-One

Another connection technique is called One-on-One. It can be effective in helping leaders make vital community connections. This connection method is also used in my own efforts to develop a better sense of community among charitable organizations and the people they serve in my area of Iowa. It is meant to make others feel more connected to the greater community.

The definition of a One-on-One consists of a 30-minute meeting designed to peel away layers that separate us in casual conversations. The idea is to discover another person by finding out who they are, what matters to them, and what motivates them while listening for talents, interests, passions, and frustrations. Even the concept of setting up a meeting just to get to know someone is uncomfortable. But it is an extremely effective way to build relationships. Call it old-fashioned, but it works. Since the One-on-One is so essential, we have included a chart contrasting what the process is and is not.

A One-on-One...

| Is | Is Not |
| --- | --- |
| Probing | Prying |
| Interrupting | Chit chat; playing it safe |
| Vulnerability | Therapy; spill guts out |
| Agitation | Irritating |
| Story | Philosophy |
| An action | Time to tell stories for no reason |
| Public relationship | Friendship |
| Why? | What? How? |

*Continued on next page.*

| Conversation | Interview; speeches |
|---|---|
| Stirring your imagination | Draining your energy |
| Mostly listening | Mostly talking |
| Finding out reason for public action | Time to gossip |

Source: Adapted from the Industrial Areas Foundation, a national community organizing network established in 1940 by Saul Alinsky.

At the end of the exercise, participants record reflections, key points, and important stories. For many people, intentional communication is a challenge and not a natural process. But the results for leaders can be powerful and rewarding. In fact, this method can be used in any organization—even families—where the goal is to develop stronger relationships, where people know each other on a deeper level. See the Workshop Suggestions section at the end of this chapter for more specific instructions on conducting a One-on-One session.

## The Circle Way

Christina Baldwin, author of *The Circle Way* (2010) and *Storycatcher* (2005), advocates "storycatching" as a method to have people share their stories and connect. While this method includes telling the story, it also involves creating the space for "catching"—making the time for sharing the story. It is through these stories that connections and caring occur. Story beginnings can be questions such as:

- Tell us a story about your work.
- What inspires you to get up in the morning?
- When did you know you wanted to go into this field?

According to Baldwin, we are looking for connections to one another—a thread of commonality. That's why we all personalize our offices with meaningful items. "People fill their cubicles with items that reflect their stories so we might ask them to share their stories," Baldwin told me.

The circle, or council, is an ancient form of meeting that has gathered human beings into respectful conversation for thousands of years. The circle has served as the foundation for many cultures. What transforms a meeting into a circle, Baldwin says, is the willingness of people to shift from informal socializing or opinionated discussion into a receptive attitude of thoughtful speaking and deep listening, and to embody and practice specific circle structures. See more on using the Circle Way at the end of this chapter.

As I explain in the next chapter, there is so much we can learn from young children. In a short time, children develop friendships fast. They don't have the defensiveness and insecurities that inhibit most adults until they "learn" to have them. That is why we need to have "ice breakers" to get adults mingling and out of our comfort zones.

In order to reclaim a sense of community, we have to realize that everything and everyone is connected to everything and everyone else. We can't treat peers in ways different from how we treat subordinates. People at all levels need to be empowered to perform at their full capacity. Christina Baldwin emphasized how she has learned from the Circle Way that the flatter the hierarchy, the smarter the company becomes. This tends to go against the norms in society. A perfect example is Donald Trump on the television show *The Apprentice*. The show reinforces that "we have to be the top of the pile."

Baldwin told me that where they have fostered circle work, people thrive. "We teach people the skills to be collaborative."

Yet, shallowness is fostered by technology. According to Twitter, we are supposed to communicate in 140 characters. This is extremely limiting for purposeful conversation and dialogue. It does not encourage building relationships where people trust one another.

## Community With the Environment

*Ishmael: An Adventure of Mind and Spirit,* a novel by Daniel Quinn (1992), consists almost entirely of the dialogue between a narrator and a gorilla. Ishmael (the gorilla) guides the narrator in learning how to "see" some of our deepest assumptions—assumptions shared by most modern societies that are so taken for granted that it is almost impossible for us to realize their impact. Ishmael's teachings through Socratic questioning helps us think about the land-hungry hierarchical societies—which he called Takers—that overwhelmed the ecologically healthy hunter-gatherer cultures—which he calls Leavers. The Taker culture that produced modern civilization does not see man as part of nature, but as separate from and superior to the rest of creation. It's a book that can change the way you see the world.

The book was part of a course offered by the Foundations for Leadership Program in Boston, sponsored by the Society for Organizational Learning (SoL) and facilitated by Peter Senge. SoL is a global community of corporations, researchers, and consultants dedicated to the "interdependent development of people and their institutions." It fit perfectly with a theme of urging leaders to forge vital connections with our shared environment. As Senge noted during the conference, "We consider the living universe around us as nothing more than 'natural resources' that exist solely for us to take and use. We must start now to think differently about this."

Another way of thinking about community is our connection in a larger sense—being connected to the environment. We are hearing more leaders talk about the triple bottom line: people, profits, and planet. After all, it is hard to focus on our immediate working community and the community we live in without thinking about the health of the environment shared by all.

A related story involves Ray Anderson, the founder and CEO of Interface Incorporated. In *Mid-Course Correction* (1996) he describes his "epiphany" and personal journey that led him to an organizational mission of leaving a "zero footprint" on the Earth. He emphasized his commitment to the environment and why other leaders should take up the challenge. "We are each and every one part of the web of life," he told me. "We have a choice on our brief visit on Earth. We can choose to hurt or to help." He says he chose to help.

As to why more CEOs don't take up the challenge, he said the change does require a fundamental change in leadership approach. "Why don't more CEOs get it?" he said, "If not with their minds, then with their hearts? This takes a fundamental shift in thinking—one mind at a time." After all, he said "What CEO stands before his maker and talks about shareholder value?"

Leaders who don't value community and connection are often afraid of vulnerability, connectedness, and depth of relationships. Richard Leider said it this way: "Mattering equals meaning. The perception that we're important to others, that we belong to a tribe or community, is important. Mattering matters."

Building community does not happen naturally, but depends on leaders making intentional decisions to do so. Systems and processes have to be changed in order to create a culture that builds, sustains, and rewards community building.

When I think of community, I am reminded of a line in *Traveling Mercies: Some Thoughts on Faith* (1999) by Anne Lamott. She quotes something she saw at a Jewish Theological Seminary. It said, "A human life is like a single letter of the alphabet. It can be meaningless. Or it can be part of a great meaning." Community helps us find our sense of purpose and a meaning that is greater than ourselves.

If we want to build a sense of community, we have to be intentional about making it happen. It does not automatically happen. Leaders are responsible for creating a culture where people want to work—healthy workplaces. Ray Rood, founder and CEO of The Genysys Group, said it this way, "The future belongs to those who dare to envision the future, treat their vision as fact, and take responsibility for translating their vision into reality."

Jim Autry, a former senior vice president of the Meredith Corporation and president of its magazine group, uses poetry to emphasize the messages he believes are important for leaders to understand. I use several of his poems in my courses and workshops, and "Threads" from his book *Love and Profit: The Art of Caring Leadership* (1991) is one of my favorites. Below is an excerpt from "Threads" that reminds us of the significance of connections:

> *Listen.*
> *in every office*
> *you hear the threads*
> *of love, and joy, and fear, and guilt,*

*the cries for celebration and reassurance,*
*and somehow you know that connecting those threads*
*is what you are supposed to do*
*and business takes care of itself.*

## Workshop Suggestions

### 1. Community Activities

*Description:* This exercise involves making participants build community by planning activities that bring people together.

*Instructions:* The purpose is to plan events that bring people together in community. Examples could be bowling or square dancing. These activities do not require talent. Everyone can participate and join in the fun. Not only do these events bring people together, but they facilitate getting to know different sides of people. These activities are inclusive and also relieve stress.

### 2. Talking Stick

*Description:* This exercise creates community by giving the "floor" to the person who is holding the "stick."

*Instructions:* The only person talking is the person with the talking "stick" (pen, pencil, rock, coin). Use a stick or any object that can be passed around to structure talking and listening. People talk when they feel moved to do so. Therefore, people don't have to go in any order. When they are talking, everyone is to listen—not ask questions or make comments.

### 3. Storytelling

*Description:* This purpose of this exercise is to be intentional about sharing stories.

*Instructions:* Start and end meetings with stories. Start each meeting with a story "check-in." Ask people to spend one to two minutes sharing a personal story. Leave it open and flexible so that people feel comfortable sharing. At the end of the meeting, close with a "check-out" such as: What did you learn? What are you personally taking out of this meeting?

### 4. The Circle Way

*Description:* This exercise is a new structure for holding a meeting that encourages participation and gives every voice respect.

*Instructions:* Gather in the middle of the room in a circle. Meetings are held in a circle to encourage deep listening and active engagement by all participants. Similar to pieces of a jigsaw puzzle, people fit together as a collaborative field—not a competitive one. In a circle, it is possible to hear and see everyone. Basic guidelines for calling a circle can be found at http://www.peerspirit.com. The use of agreements in a circle allows all members to have a free and profound exchange, to respect a diversity of views, and to share responsibility for the well-being and direction of the group. Agreements often used include:

- We will hold stories or personal material in confidentiality.

- We listen to each other with compassion and curiosity.

- We ask for what we need and offer what we can.

- We agree to employ a group guardian to watch our need, timing, and energy.

- We agree to pause at a signal, and to call for that signal when we feel the need to pause.

## Personal Development Suggestions

1. **Ask Questions**

*Description:* This exercise is to help people get to know one another better.

*Instructions:* Relationships form when we know each other. A great way to get to know people and to start conversations is to ask questions. Asking questions puts our focus on them rather than talking about ourselves. Relationships help us build community in organizations, in families, and in the greater communities in which we live.

2. **One-on-One Meetings**

*Description:* This exercise involves conducting one-on-one meetings to get to know each other.

*Instructions:* Identify someone you want to get to know better. If you know the person, you might want to get to know them on a deeper level. Invite this person out for coffee. Explain that there is no agenda other than to get to know each other better. Then start asking questions about topics that are nonthreatening—interests, hobbies, activities.

## Readings

Many books can remind us of the value of building community if we are "awake" when reading them. I highly recommend reading *Ishmael: An Adventure of the Mind and Spirit* (1992) by Daniel Quinn. *The Fifth Discipline: The Art and Practice of the Learning Organization* (1994) by Peter Senge is a classic book about thinking of organizations as systems. *The Servant Leader: How to Build a Creative Team,*

*Develop Great Morale, and Improve Bottom-line Performance* (2001) by Jim Autry integrates many of the themes of this book.

Margaret Wheatley has written several books that can be used to build community, such as *Leadership and the New Science: Learning about Organization from an Orderly Universe* (1994). Since conversations are critical in building community, her book *Turning to One Another: Simple Conversations to Restore Hope to the Future* (2009) reinforces the value of creating conversations. She describes how we should change our language from one of judgment to one of curiosity. We have so much to learn from each other.

Peter Block is an expert on building community. *Community* (2008) and the book he co-authored with John McKnight, *The Abundant Community* (2010), describe how to create community in organizations, families, and neighborhoods. Christina Baldwin's *Storycatching* (2005) explains how to encourage the use of story in organization. *The Circle Way* (2010), is a great resource for designing meetings to enhance conversation and participation as a way of creating stronger community.

## What's Next?

Leaders need to model resilience and renewal to thrive through uncertainty and lead in chaos. This chapter outlines how a true sense of curiosity and creative thinking are essential, and how to effectively model a resilient attitude and mindset. The chapter includes other ways of becoming resilient in the increasingly complex world in which we live and work.

# Chapter 7

# Leaders Model Resilience

*How can organizations be creative in the absence*
*of creative and curious leaders?*
*—Betty Sue Flowers*

One of the characteristics of being a sage is staying power. A sage has endured obstacles and recognizes the importance of coping mechanisms and ways of being resilient. A clear theme that emerged among the more than 100 interviews was the significance of modeling resilience and renewal. But what exactly is resilience, and more importantly, how do leaders build their reserves of such a vital leadership skill?

Richard Boyatzis, co-author of *Resonant Leadership* (2005), told me that in working with executives he has found that renewal relies on three key elements that support being a resonant leader: mindfulness, hope, and compassion. He said that the interactions among these elements create positive emotions that enable us to remain resilient when faced with challenges; this describes the current climate leaders face. But he reminded me that developing into resonant leaders does not automatically happen without a process of intentional change that involves a learning agenda.

There is no question that learning how to model resilience is a needed practice in these uncertain times that include stress, pressure, and dissonance. If the most important person to lead is ourselves, then we need to learn new behaviors and practices that help us address these challenges. As Boyatzis and McKee (2005) conclude, "We need to focus deliberately on creating resonance within ourselves—mind, body, and spirit—and then channel our resonance to the people and groups around us" (10).

In these uncertain times, it is easy to get stuck in a trap and not know how to move forward. Robert Persig in his classic book, *Zen and the Art of Motorcycle Maintenance,* describes monkey traps as a metaphor for how easy it is to become stuck in our ways and rigid in our thoughts and behaviors (see the sidebar for the story). When this happens, it is difficult to be creative, innovative, and curious. It is only by letting go that we are set free—and can become unstuck.

# Letting Go

In Southeast Asia, monkeys are trapped and moved away from the cities because they cause too much destruction. The natives have created an ingenious way of capturing them. The trap consists of a hollowed out coconut chained to a stake. The coconut has some rice inside which can be grabbed through a small hole. The hole is big enough so that the monkey's hand can go in, but too small for his fist with rice in it to come out. The monkey reaches in and is suddenly trapped—by nothing more than his own value rigidity. He can't revalue the rice. He cannot see the freedom without rice is more valuable than capture with it.

There is a fact that this monkey should know: If he opens his hand he's free. But how is he going to discover this fact? By removing the value rigidity that rates rice above freedom. How is he going to do that? Well, he should somehow try to deliberately slow down, go over ground that he has been over before, see if things he thought were important really were important, and well, stop yanking and just stare at the coconut for a while.

Source: Excerpt from Persig, R. (2009). *Zen and the Art of Motorcycle Maintenance*. New York: Bantam Books, p. 320.

Diane Coutu provides a starting point for both individual leaders and their organizations in her 2002 *Harvard Business Review* article "How Resilience Works." According to Coutu, resilient people and organizations possess three key characteristics:

- a staunch acceptance of reality
- a deep belief supported by strong values that life is meaningful
- an ability to improvise.

A quick scan of Coutu's three points might lead you to conclude that resilient people are the most "grown up" or adult people, but we all know from experience this is not true. The most resilient people are those who have the least trouble seeing the world as it is. They view the world with a sense of wonder in a way that does not preclude changing directions when necessary. They are often the people with the most curious and childlike outlook on life.

"Children are naturally curious. It is only as we age that our natural curiosity is often replaced by ersatz wisdom masquerading as worldly sophistication. We become so certain that we know other people, and how the world works, that our ability to be pleasantly surprised and even delighted wanes, withers, or expires. Compassion, then, by definition, involves a renewal of the innate curiosity with which we were born" (McKee, Johnston, and Massimilian, 2006, 4).

In my workshops, I often point to the 1980s movie *Big* starring Tom Hanks as an extreme example of seeing the world with a new sense of curiosity. In the movie, a young boy gets his wish fulfilled "to be big" and the audience gets to see what we do in our work and personal lives in a new, hilarious, and sometimes profound way. In the movie, we witness how Hanks's sense of wonder and curiosity is appealing to other adults. People want to follow him because of his attitude and the environment he creates just by being in the space.

Another fictional example of changing perspectives is found in Matthew Kelly and Patrick Lencioni's book *The Dream Manager* (2007) about a leader and his executive team who set out to transform their organization. They actively engage a disengaged workforce by hiring a "dream manager" charged with helping employees achieve their dreams. The book poses some challenging questions that I also incorporate into my workshops including:

- What is the difference between striving for dreams and accomplishing goals?
- Do we know the dreams of the people we care about?
- Do they know our own dreams?
- How would our relationships be different if we knew people's dreams?

I ask participants to talk about their dreams and their related goals. When talking about dreams, people are consistently more inspired and engaged. It's also a good introduction to the topic of modeling resilience and renewal as a leader. While goals can feel like heavy burdens to accomplish, dreams are uplifting and this is easily seen both in how people are interacting and in their body language. When we know people's dreams, we want to help them reach them, and the process is energizing.

Unfortunately, many leaders don't understand their role as "meaning makers" and why their direct support of creative and innovative work environments is important. P.J. Mitchell, Vice President of Global Operations for IBM, positioned the organization's role this way: "How do we get young people, particularly women, to lean into the wind more? We don't provide the spaces to celebrate risk-taking and we fail to recognize that the next person builds on the experience." What leaders and their organizations need to do, Mitchell continued, is support "innovation and prudent risk taking. You can't cut your way to growth. You can't turn the motor off when the water gets choppy. In a down economy, companies are not going to survive and thrive in an environment of fear."

## Building Resilience—Five Paths

As I probed the sages about how to develop ways to survive and thrive in the ever-changing world in which we live and work, what emerged were different approaches to change our perspectives. We need to shift our mind-set so we see things differently in order to make the best decisions personally and professionally.

Many ways exist to build your leadership resilience, but here are five suggestions with a consistent track record:

- Go on a retreat.

- Get creative.

- Keep learning.

- Celebrate small wins.

- Develop a practice.

## Go on a Retreat

The most effective leaders make time for a personal retreat. The retreat can be a specific place (such as the monastery I described in chapter 2) or any escape from your usual productive activities, as long as you spend the time building your inner reserves and engaging in the process of renewal and self-care.

All this focus on the "inner self" may sound foreign to participants in a workshop or other learning activity, but you can overcome the resistance by organizing manageable "sample" retreats (see Workshop Suggestions at the end of this chapter). For those willing to do the work, these retreats can be a gateway to more formal, organized retreats such as a visit to a monastery.

Since I already participate in retreats, I use these experiences in my leadership workshops to model why it's important to make time for a personal retreat. Often, my participants can't imagine why anyone would want to spend time in a monastery for the purpose of a silent retreat. To make my case, I often relate the story of the hospice worker I met on my first retreat who spends one weekend of every month at the monastery. She told me that as the regional chaplain of a hospice network, she used the time to properly grieve for all those she had cared for in the weeks before coming to the monastery. "Since death is a part of my job," she said, "I don't have the time that is needed to grieve for each person who has died. Mentally, I wrap them up and put them in the trunk of my car until the next weekend at the Abbey when I have the time to grant each person the time they deserve."

The Abbey retreat is now part of my life. I return to the Abbey at least once a year and Father Jonah, the current Guest Master, is a friend, confidant, and one of my life coaches. Once the participants hear my personal story, they are less hesitant to embark on their own personal journey.

## Get Creative

Resilience is also built and maintained through creative expression. It doesn't matter how it's expressed as long as the activity moves the leaders you are trying to motivate out of their typical ways of thinking or approaching problems or issues.

You have probably attended or perhaps even performed in a talent show put on by an organization, club, or association. The idea is to draw on the talent "in the room" to entertain the assembled group. It's a great way to draw out the creativity in any group, even a group of leaders.

For example, one reason I look forward to attending the annual Organizational Behavior Teaching Conference (OBTC) is for the event's talent show. In fact, one professor of psychology is so good as a stand-up comedian that his "act" is one of the most highly anticipated events of the conference.

Not only do these talent shows help people get to know one another better, but they also serve as a way for leaders to reenergize and model resilience by demonstrating facets of our lives beyond work. In fact, I often devote the last class in a course (or this could be incorporated into a workshop) participants demonstrating or explaining their creativity activity (explained in the next section). This has been well received and is another way of building community.

I have also integrating dancing—any kind of dancing—into courses and workshops. Dancing is an excellent metaphor for discussing when to lead and when to follow. I bring in a dance instructor to teach us about ballroom dancing or lead us in square dancing. And square dancing, in particular, is a nonthreatening form of expression that does not take any natural talent or skill. After a session on dancing, we talk about body language and listening to what is not said. The discussion usually covers topics such as confidence, relationships, and stress management.

## Keep Learning

Continuous learning also supports resilience in leaders and models a productive pathway for the workforce. Jim Collins advocates keeping a "to-learn list" as well as a "to-do list" and a "stop-doing list," with an admonition to use the time gained from checking off items on your "stop doing" to add to your "to-learn" list. Since we only have 24 hours in a day, it is a matter of being intentional about how we allocate our behaviors in the context of time.

All of my leadership workshops and courses stress the value of learning, and I require participants to learn a new skill outside of the class called a "creativity activity." The activity can be anything from artistic endeavors to engaging or re-engaging with a hobby or passion they'd abandoned. During the course, the participants are required to keep a journal about the time spent doing this activity and report on the experience and what they've learned. We have a talent show at the end of the course where participants share what they did and the difference it made in their life.

The main point of the exercise is for participants to "feel" the difference of integrating this type of activity in their schedule. Since life is more than work, making time for creative endeavors should be a priority that helps in resilience and renewal. Learning something new can be simultaneously challenging and energizing while also changing one's perspective (see the sidebar, "Look at the View").

# Look at the View

Another form of renewal is changing our perspective. Anna Quindlen, in *A Short Guide to a Happy Life*, tells the personal story of how she found one of her best teachers on the boardwalk at Coney Island several years ago.

It was December and she was working on a story about how the homeless suffer in the winter. She sat down on the edge of the boardwalk next to a man who told her how he slept in a church when the temperature was cold and panhandled the crowd during the summer months. He would hide from the police in the Tilt-A-Whirl and some of the other rides. But he told her that most of the time he stayed on the boardwalk, facing the water, and when it got cold he had to wear his newspapers after he read them. She asked him why he didn't go to one of the shelters. She asked him why he didn't check himself into the hospital for detox. And he stared out at the ocean and said, "Look at the view, young lady. Look at the view."

And Quindlen learned to try to remember to look at the view. "Words of wisdom from a man with not a dime in his pocket, no place to go, nowhere to be. Look at the view."

Retreats are a place to remind us to look at the view. But when we are conscious of our perspective, wherever we are we can be intentional about reminding ourselves to "look at the view."

Source: Quindlen, A. (2000). *A Short Guide to a Happy Life*. New York: Random House.

---

## Celebrate Small Wins

Learning to model resilience and renewal may sound overwhelming—similar to starting a new exercise routine—but the key is to start by taking small, incremental steps and celebrating the "small wins." Karl Weick, a professor of psychology at the University of Michigan, coined the phrase "small wins" as a way of reframing the scale of social problems. According to Weick (1984), "A small win is a concrete, complete, implemented outcome ... When we recast larger problems into smaller, less arousing problems, people can identify a series of controllable opportunities of modest size that produce visible results that can be gathered into solutions" (43). Weick attributes the success of Alcoholics Anonymous to the fact that people are not asked to abstain for the rest of their lives, but rather to stay sober for a day at a time or even an hour.

The concept of small wins can be life changing because the momentum of celebrating progress can lead to higher levels of motivation and a sense of hope and optimism. Each success (small win) increases confidence and momentum. This concept is pertinent in these uncertain times when situations seem too complicated and massive to address, such as several recent natural disasters.

# Making a Difference

This classic children's story illustrates the power of small wins. Hundreds of starfish have washed up on a beach. A young girl is carefully putting one starfish and then another back in the water. Observing this with amusement, a man comments that her effort is futile because she can't possibly save all of them. She replies, holding up a starfish, "But I can make a difference to this one."

Making a difference, step by small step, separates long-term winners, who have the confidence to achieve their goals, from those who always seem to fall short. Instead of feeling overwhelmed by the magnitude of the problems, social entrepreneurs identify achievable actions and get started.

Small wins aren't as dramatic as big bold strokes, but they can be more effective and more fulfilling, because each success increases confidence.

Source: Kanter, R.M. (2005). "Get Involved—You'll Be Happy That You Did." *Miami Herald*, October 6, 2005.

When I share the concept of "small wins" in classes and workshops, I first ask people to name what would be a "big win" for them. People typically respond by saying things such as marriage, graduation, having children, or their favorite sports team winning a Super Bowl or the World Series. Then I ask them, "How often do these big wins happen?" The usual answer is, "Not very often." So if we live for the big wins, we often live with disappointment. Celebrating small wins keeps us positive and hopeful.

When I describe small wins, I usually reference the movie *Groundhog Day*. In the movie, Bill Murray's character asks a question for which there is no one right answer: "What would you do if you were stuck in one place and every day was the same and nothing mattered?" I use this question to start a conversation about the meaning of life and one's individual view of it. In the movie, Murray goes through various stages of feeling trapped, depressed, and desperate because there is no tomorrow.

Former *Boston Globe* columnist Ellen Goodman, in her book *Value Judgments* (1993), summarized the movie best by saying that finally Murray arrives at the "not-so-profound-but-still-pretty-rare realization that he can change his world by changing himself" (333). Instead of feeling stuck, leaders need to develop practices that help them re-energize and renew. And the key is to start small and to celebrate the small wins along the way.

Another method I have used to illustrate the concept of small wins is to show the film, *The Man Who Planted Trees*, based on the book by the same title by Jean Giono that was first published in 1953. *The Man Who Planted Trees* tells the story of a shepherd who takes it upon himself to patiently plant thousands of trees one by one until he has single-handedly transformed his arid surroundings into a thriving oasis. Undeterred by two World Wars, and without any thought of personal reward, the shepherd tirelessly sows his seeds and acorns with the greatest care.

As if by magic, a landscape that seemed condemned grows green again. By viewing each acorn as a "small win," the story illustrates how breaking an overwhelming task down into small achievable actions can lead to accomplishing great things. You witness momentum building and attitudes changing. It is a parable for all ages and an inspiring testament to the power of one person who celebrates the small wins.

## Excerpt From *The Man Who Planted Trees*

When I reflect that one man, armed only with his own physical and moral resources, was able to cause this land of Canaan to spring from the wasteland, I am convinced that in spite of everything, humanity is admirable. But when I compute the unfailing greatness of spirit and the tenacity of benevolence that it must have taken to achieve this result, I am taken with an immense respect for that old and unlearned peasant who was able to complete a work worthy of God.

Source: Giona, J. (1953). *The Man Who Planted Trees*. London: Owen (Peter) Ltd.

## Developing a Practice

Developing a "practice" is a way of relieving stress and anxiety. It is something that informs the decisions we make, is constant, and can't be taken away.

While the principles of leadership often appear to be common sense, common sense is not that common. The lessons I learned from the sages are easy to understand, but difficult to implement, since repeated behaviors become habits and habits are hard to change without intention and consistent practice.

Jim Kouzes, co-author of *Leadership Challenge* (2012) and other leadership books, emphasized to me how most leaders don't consider what they do as a skill needing practice. He said this was the first thing that people in influential positions need to understand—that leadership needs to be practiced and improvement only happens when honest feedback is given.

Malcolm Gladwell reports in *Outliers* (2008) that it takes most people 10,000 hours to become excellent at a sport, instrument, or skill. Professional musicians and athletes hire coaches who are expected to give them honest feedback for improvement. Yet, leaders often operate in a vacuum without any feedback.

Jim Hunter, author of *The Servant* (1998), described his principles as undoing and unlearning old habits. He told me, "We are bundles of habits, and leaders need to create a culture to help people learn new habits, in order to continuously improve." He outlined three specific steps to making changes and then practicing these new habits:

1. **Foundation:** Setting the standard. And as Covey says, "Begin with the end in mind."

2. **Feedback:** Based on 360-degree feedback, understand where the gaps are between desired behaviors and actual behaviors.

3. **Friction:** Healthy tension. This is the accountability piece. Feedback is shared with people who know you. Then you

select two areas in which you want to grow and set specific and measurable plans to get there. A progress report is given on a regular basis to a peer group.

Hunter emphasized how this process is also a practice in humility for three reasons. He said that we all have gaps—no one has arrived as the perfect leader or person. People know your gaps because it was a group who reported the gaps. And then it is time to work together as a team on our gaps. He said that his process is about character and moral development so that we evolve into better leaders and people (see the sidebar).

## Renewal for Resilience

The current leadership deficit in America is far more serious than our fiscal deficit. The demand for healthy-minded, wise, and ethical leaders far exceeds the supply. Many young people possess the raw materials of long-distance leadership—intelligence, drive, organizational skills, and the will to lead—yet never make it to maturity. And, as we've seen, many of their mature counterparts derail or self-destruct at the height of their success. Both of these failures are due to a larger failure to identify and promote the most fundamental qualities of leadership—which are also the qualities of the self-renewing person (p. 233).

Source: O'Neil, J. (1993). *The Paradox of Success*. New York: G.P. Putnam's Sons.

Developing ways to be resilient is essential for leaders and the rest of us to be effective. The formula is easy to verbalize, but hard to implement. Be curious rather than judgmental. Find ways to stimulate your curiosity and seek out people who stimulate your thinking. Take a personal retreat to listen to your inner voice and to get grounded in what matters most. Strive to integrate creativity because it makes life more interesting and enjoyable. Take time to learn some new skill and unlearn habits that no longer support your personal story.

Finally, remember to look at the view (see the sidebar earlier in this chapter). "Failing to acknowledge our blessings isolates and disconnects us from the larger contexts of life, from the community of feeling….Gratitude teaches us that interdependence does not mean loss of identity or giving up control" (O'Neil, 1993, 158). Gratitude is a way of thinking and living that influences our behaviors in positive ways and at the same time builds resilience.

## Workshop Suggestions

1. **Talent Show**

*Description:* This exercise is an event where people can showcase their talents.

*Instructions:* Create a regular opportunity for people to demonstrate their talents on a volunteer basis. Allow a wide variety of talents such as readings, singing, playing instruments, acting, or even juggling. Provide the environment where people can relax and be entertained by their peers. The rewards are too numerous to list, but imaginations and creativity soars along with relationships as people realize hidden talents and common interests.

2.  **Let's Dance**

*Description:* This exercise is to demonstrate how dancing is a good metaphor for learning about leading versus following.

*Instructions:* Bring in a dance instructor to teach the group the basics of ballroom dancing or to lead the group in square dancing. Have the partners take turns leading and following so each gets to be in each role. After the session, talk about how it felt to lead versus follow. What were their observations about their partner? About themselves?

## Personal Development Suggestions

1.  **Creativity Activity**

*Description:* The purpose is to learn something new that is creative or to make time for an activity that you used to enjoy and have not done for quite some time.

*Instructions:* Make an intentional decision to learn something new that would fit under the broad umbrella of "creativity." This activity can be something that you used to do in the past that you would like to revisit, or it can be something totally new. The goal is to "get out of your comfort zone" and do something that might enrich your life by reenergizing your spirit and raising your energy level. All of these positive consequences can be transferred to the workplace.

2.  **Find a Role Model**

*Description:* The purpose is to intentionally seek out someone who is living life in a way that appeals to you—a life of renewal and resilience.

*Instructions:* Focus on someone in your life whom you have followed in the past or would be happy to follow. Why would you follow them? The conclusion is we all know a good leader we would follow—living or not, man or woman or animal, mortal or immortal, real or mythic, even a character in a novel. What are they doing that renews their spirit? What do they do to be resilient?

### 3. Plan a Personal Retreat

*Description:* The purpose of a retreat is to get in touch with yourself. The time is focused on a "recovery of the self"—the complete whole self. The goal is to spend time being in the presence of one's own company.

*Instructions:* Find a place where you can get away from the pressures and tensions of daily life—where you can feel relaxed and unhurried. A retreat might be a day, a weekend, or more. It might be spending time in a natural setting, a monastery, or some secluded location. Questions you might ask during retreat include:

- Are you prepared to meet some aspects of your shadow?
- Is play feeling like work?
- Have you set aside some time to explore questions of meaning?
- Is solitude comfortable for you?
- Are rituals in place to support deeper explorations of your life?
- Is there professional help available if you want or need it?

### 4. Build Support for Renewal

*Description:* The purpose of this exercise is to develop a support system and network for helping build our resilience.

*Instructions:* The higher we go in the organization, the more we tend to live in a "fishbowl," where it feels as though everyone is watching us and we are all alone. Relationships remind us that we are not alone and that we need to help each other confront workplace pressures that manifest as burnout, stress, and unhealthy behaviors. Identify people who are part of your support system and intentionally thank them for their advice and support.

5.  A "Stop-Doing" List and "To-Learn" List

*Description:* The purpose is to focus on learning rather than just doing—or being busy.

*Instructions:* Since we only have 24 hours in a day, we need to stop doing things to find time to learn new things. Make a list of the tasks you need to stop doing so that you have time for learning something new.

## Readings

In addition to the books mentioned in this chapter, I recommend *Becoming a Resonant Leader: Develop Your Emotional Intelligence, Renew Your Relationships, and Sustain Your Effectiveness.* This book by Annie McKee, Richard Boyatzis, and Frances Johnston is an excellent resource. It is written as a workbook to be used individually or in a workshop setting. Karl Weick's classic article on "Small Wins" (1984) is often cited in books as a must read for understanding the power of celebrating the small wins to help with any problem that can seem overwhelming. When we focus on the small wins, usually motivation is enhanced, stress is easier to manage, and hope and optimism overcome despair. As stated in this chapter, I recommend using the book or film *The Man Who Planted Trees* (2004) as a way to illustrate this concept.

Julia Cameron is an authority on creativity. *The Complete Artist's Way: Creativity as a Spiritual Practice* (2007) is an extensive book of activities to stimulate creativity. Since dancing is a creative venture, I recommend watching a film about dancing before bringing in a dance instructor, if time permits. This helps participants make connections between the fundamentals of dance and leadership. Some films I have used include *Madhot Ballroom* (2005), *Strictly Dancing* (1992), *Shall We Dance* (2004), *Save the Last Dance* (2001), and *Top Hat* (1935).

## What's Next?

Leaders have an absolute obligation to create healthy work environments. The next chapter includes specific examples how award-winning organizations and their leaders have built healthy, productive work environments while repairing toxic ones.

# Chapter 8

# Leaders Create Healthy Work Environments

*My purpose is to nurture and inspire the human spirit. I start with myself and then work to do this with others.*

—Howard Behar

President Truman famously kept a sign on his desk that said "The Buck Stops Here." Truman's unambiguous acceptance of responsibility for the consequences of every decision is a concept endorsed by all 100 sages and other experts I interviewed for this book. This responsibility extends to the overall work environment created for the organizations they lead.

Jeffrey Pfeffer said in *The Human Equation: Building Profits by Putting People First* (1998) that he believes employers who treat people poorly experience low rates of productivity, high rates of turnover, and invariably complain about the death of loyalty and the death of talent. But Ann Coombs told me that "Loyalty is not dead; it is being killed by toxic workplaces that drive people away."

Pfeffer defines a toxic workplace as "a place where people come to work so they can make enough money so they can leave it." Coombs defines a toxic workplace as one "without honest human relationships." If a toxic working environment exists, the responsibility is directly traceable to the leader at the top, just as surely as the leader at the top is connected to the engaged and productive work environment they create.

Through my research, I discovered successful leaders working hard to create healthy workplaces, and I asked for specifics on how they were doing this. Doing this work is challenging, but it's one of the best investments leaders can make in their organizations. Interestingly, my research reinforced what Kim Cameron reported in *Positive Leadership: Strategies for Extraordinary Performance*. He concluded that there are three important activities for promoting a positive climate among employees—compassion, forgiveness, and gratitude. His research found that "companies that scored higher on these activities were found to have performed significantly better than others in a study of organizations across 16 different industry groups" (Cameron, 2012, p. 32).

## Toxic Workplace Environment

When I visualize the effects of a toxic workplace, I visualize a tree. Trees are survivors at all costs. They remain standing through storms and droughts. It takes a lot to kill them. But if you put poison on the soil surrounding the tree, that poison will seep into the roots and then be pulled into the tree itself. Eventually, the tree will be so weakened that it will stop growing. Its leaves will turn yellow and drop off. In time, the smallest puff of wind will knock it down.

In toxic workplaces, the poison is spread through word of mouth, and through the way the company's products and services are perceived by its customers, suppliers, associates, and allies. Eventually, some emergency—perhaps a major interruption in the cash flow or the loss of a key order—will bring the business to a crisis point.

Source: Coombs, A. (2004). *The Living Workplace: Soul, Spirit, and Success in the 21st Century.* Toronto: Warwick Publishing Inc., pp. 45-46

Robert "Skip" Backus, CEO of the Omega Institute, told me this about the leader's responsibility to create healthy work environments when I interviewed him a few years ago:

*"The goal is to create a working environment that honors individuals and brings a sense of presence, responsibility, and integrity into the moment. At Omega, we want to have a sense of peace and commitment in the environment, so everything we do is intentional, from providing good organic food to no telephones in the rooms. We think the work environment should be a representation of our whole life since we spend so much time at work. Therefore, work should reflect our life values."*

And Darlyne Bailey, co-author of *Sustaining our Spirits: Women Leaders Thriving for Today and Tomorrow* (2008), described leadership responsibility to me this way: "Leaders have to create the environment by starting little fires throughout the organization. One leader in an organization can put some light out there, but may not be able to make it as bright as it can be as if she or he went out and tried to light up others in the organization."

Finally, Fasha Mahjoor, founder and president of Phenomenex, a chemical specialty firm in California celebrated for its culture of spirit at work, had this to say about his style of leadership that built the environment at his organization:

> *"I attribute all of our success to our people and that is a direct reflection of our culture. It is critical to create a culture of ownership so that people understand their impact. If you don't create work and life balance, how do they stay in the game showing up every day and performing at their best level? I describe our culture as vivacious, energetic, optimistic, and a positive force for people. It is a culture of good business because it is good for people in every way. Our goal is to create an environment that is worthy of their presence."*

## Happy Workers Equals Better Productivity

"Being able to be truly happy at work is one of the keys to being happy in life," says Heidi Golledge, CEO and co-founder of CareerBliss, an online career database. Yet, according to research done by The Gallup Organization (*Gallup Business Journal*, 2013) and National Business Research Institute (www.nbrii.com), workers have never been more disengaged and dissatisfied at work. Their research revealed only one in three employees is engaged at work, and this costs the American economy up to $350 billion a year in lost productivity. Specifically, 55 percent of all U.S. workers are not engaged and 16 percent are actively disengaged. This means 71 percent of the Americans who go to work every day are not engaged in their roles and responsibilities. This also means that American businesses are operating at one-third of their capacity. Not only is this a significant lost opportunity for productivity, but a lost opportunity for employees to grow and to be happy.

The NBRI concluded that executives have significant influence on the engagement levels of all employees in the organization. Executives need to develop high levels of trust, communicate clearly, and create a culture that fuels high levels of performance and engagement. On a managerial level, they recommend managers spend time coaching for employee growth, building relationships of trust, and getting to know their staff as individuals.

A great deal of research (CareerBliss, 2012) has been conducted on how the happiest companies boost morale and the bottom line. Here are some of the conclusions:

- There is a strong correlation between happiness and meaning; having a meaningful impact on the world around you is actually a better predictor of happiness than many other things thought to make you happy.

- When policies ensure people get feedback and praise for a job well done.

- When employees are considered as people first, workers second, policies exist that focus on their well-being as individuals.

- Emphasize work-life integration, not just "balance."

"When you 'get' that employees are human beings first and worker bees second, you say something about their worth. Companies with happily engaged employees ... hire people with a capacity to care for one another, foster connectedness at every level of the company, give an inspiring vision not laced with BS platitudes, but about real possibilities.

You want to work in these places because they make you feel purposeful, connected, and valued" (Dishman, 2013). My research reinforced these findings. The most effective leaders create healthy work environments, and specific ways on how they do this are described in this chapter.

## Which Companies Are Doing Something Right?

Every year *Fortune* compiles a list of the best companies to work for based on employee surveys. There is an interesting trend in their list: Many of them are privately held, where the bottom line does not drive all decisions for the benefit of stockholders. According to an article by Paul La Monica on CNNMoney.com (January, 2010), in 2010, four of the top five companies were private. In fact, nine of the top 20 Best Companies were privately held, and 40 of the top 100 do not have stock that you can buy and sell on the NYSE or Nasdaq. On this list, there were also 15 nonprofits, two partnerships, and one cooperative. The remaining 42 companies are publicly traded companies.

To drive this point home, Bob Marx, a professor of management at the University of Massachusetts, adapted the story of "driving the bus" from Daniel Goleman's book *Emotional Intelligence* (1995). He points out that the goal of the leader is to create a community "on the bus" so that when people "get off the bus," they have a different feeling than when they got on. Marx even reinforces this concept in his classes by giving his participants a key chain as a reminder that they need to pay attention to how they ultimately choose to "drive the bus."

## Creating Meaningful Workplaces

Many of the senior leaders I interviewed for this book led organizations that had received the International Spirit at Work Award (now referred to as the International Faith and Spirit at Work Awards, from the Tyson Center for Faith and Spirituality in the Workplace at the University of Arkansas). Interestingly, most of the companies are privately held, and this was pointed out to me during the interviews. Many of the leaders indicated it is sometimes more difficult to create meaningful workplaces when the focus is completely on the bottom line and where leaders have less personal freedom to allocate resources in these ways. Perhaps that's why these leaders tended to focus on what matters most and why they have worked so hard to create a holistic workplace culture. They created healthy cultures by paying attention to the reward systems; providing spaces for mind, body, and spirit; and by assessing the culture to determine if reality matched the desired culture.

Howard Behar, former CEO of Starbucks International, explained the importance of creating healthy workplaces this way: "We need to appeal to people's instincts. How would you like to be led? Most people want to be involved, empowered, and cared about... But we get into power positions and forget all of this. Servant leadership is not the norm because we are so used to people telling us what do to that when we get in the leadership position, we tell them what to do."

A strong theme among the leaders I interviewed was that creating a healthy culture—one in which people bring their whole selves to work (mind, body, and spirit)—started at the top. Senior leaders need to be the driving force for not only creating, but for maintaining the culture. Several of the organizations reported that the journey to transform the culture was a reflection of the personal journey of the leader's transformation. Once leaders were on board and had the vision for the culture, the momentum trickled down throughout the organization.

An interesting point about creating healthy cultures is that data collected by companies living these healthy organizational values reported decreased turnover, higher retention, and increased customer satisfaction. That is why many of the leaders talked about "hiring for fit" as key to maintaining a healthy culture. For example, Susan Shors, Chief Culture Officer of Eileen Fisher Incorporated, said, "We get the best people. We are a better company when we are made up of engaged, thoughtful, and wise people. Our hiring process is a long process. Each candidate meets with teams of people and are put on a six-month temporary status to see if the fit works."

Other benefits to a healthy culture include greater engagement, creativity, and less unresolved conflict. As one leader noted, "When people have purpose and meaning, they feel valued and are less stressed."

However, the road to a healthier environment is not always easy, and may take time and resources to get an entire workforce onboard. As Judy Hodgson, Senior Vice President of Organizational Development at PeaceHealth told me, "While this culture is easy to support philosophically, it is hard to walk the talk. You have to stay with it because it does matter. You have to be like a terrier and stick with it."

The leaders I interviewed from these companies had identified core values to guide behaviors. Some of the most common values mentioned were trust, honesty, and authenticity. Susan Beck, Executive Director of Hearthstone Global Foundation, a home construction company, told me every meeting includes some review of their core values, and that these values are clearly posted on signs and other physical reminders throughout the organization (see the sidebar for some sample company visions).

# Company Vision and Values Examples

CLEAN's service is so superb that our customers love working with us. Our dolphins teach us to live as one with nature, spread joy and harmony in the world, and to ride on the waves of laughter.

The habitat and behaviors of dolphins are a basis for staff rules and behaviors in the company. The analogy in the company brochure documents the importance of and desire for sustainability:

Honesty and trust: Dolphins live together in a group. They live their communal life in harmoniously regular cycles. With their special charisma, they show us humans a kind of honesty and trust and make us feel good.

Individuality and sense of community: Dolphins superbly combine their pronounced individuality with a strong sense of community. They learn from each other, provide mutual support to each other and are seen as helpful and friendly creatures.

Intelligence and social competence: Dolphins are very intelligent creatures. In addition to intuition and social competence, they have the ability to adapt to new situations and find solutions to problems.

Health and environment: Dolphins are creatures with a positive attitude to life. They are considerate of the community and work towards a healthy and natural balance of their surroundings.

Partnership and cohesion: Dolphins develop strong bonds with each other and help each other. They are able to recognize when one of their fellows needs their support and are immediately on hand to provide it.

Source: Direct excerpt from CLEAN SERVICEPOWER, an award-winning company in Germany.

---

Another example of a set of core values comes from Hearthstone Homes, Inc., a home construction firm in Omaha, Nebraska. As you review these values, notice how they reinforce the themes in this book.

- **Spirituality:** We honor our connectedness to each other and practice the principles of compassion, generosity, and service that help us define who we are and what we contribute.

- **Integrity:** We look, see, tell the truth, and take authentic action.

- **Nurturance:** We create a supportive environment that promotes interdependence.

- **Continuous learning**: We encourage growth and development in our relationships.

- **Courage:** We acknowledge our fears and choose to move beyond them.

For Hearthstone, these are not just values posted on a wall. They allocate significant funds for training and development. For example, they have a comprehensive program for personal growth and applied "coaching" that is integrated into their daily practices. The program is provided in Sacramento, California and includes four courses that are progressive in nature and last four days each. The program is available for all of their associates and their significant others. By including significant others in the training, they understand that work is a part of home and home is a part of work. Susan Beck told me that "when one person is growing, it is important the other person has the same opportunity to grow so that they grow together."

This program is also part of their recruiting process. Prior to being hired, the person is invited to attend the first course at the company's expense as a further means of determining the fit between the person's values and the culture of the company. This reflects Hearthstone's commitment to training and hiring the "right" people.

J.-Robert Ouimet, President and CEO of Holding OCB Inc., Cordon Bleu International Inc., and Ouimet-Tomasso Inc., told me he creates an engaged, productive, and trusting work environment by sponsoring testimonial sessions twice a year. This is a time when people can share with others what is on their mind. It is almost an "open mic" time for people to have the floor and share their story. He said even the ritual of doing this tells an important story. It is a time of solidarity when people are listening to others. There tends to be a repetition of values because of how the stories touch on subjects in the workplace, and repetition deepens the impression made. According to Ouimet, this has been a transforming experience that contributes to the culture he is trying to nurture and nourish.

At Prairie View Incorporated, Tamera Herl, Director of Expressive Therapies, implemented a wall mural tradition that allows employees to express their feelings about working for the organization. Herl described how the organization assesses the environment in creative ways. For example, employees were encouraged to create a giant mural by designing something on burlap that reflects their response to the question: How does it feel to be here? To work here?

The mural created represents a collective visual based on employees' perspectives. It tells a story and communicates something about the company to everyone who sees it.

A few years ago, I was conducting a series of leadership workshops for mid-level leaders at a Midwestern manufacturer during a time of reorganization and change. To assess the environment, I asked participants to draw a picture that reflected how they felt about the current organizational culture.

The illustrations were telling. One person drew a cliff with people jumping off into the water. Another person drew an ocean with big and rough waves. And some of the drawings were even more negative and graphic. It was clear that most of them felt as if the culture was being torn apart piece by piece and the organizational tapestry was disintegrating.

In the workshop, we discussed how many organizations devote very few resources to those who remain after large-scale organizational change. We also discussed why those who leave become "survivors" because they got out of the organization and those who stay become "victims" because they often feel stuck in an unhealthy culture. Our conclusion was that the best internal environments are created when a balance of worker investment and dependence on an organization is maintained. That is, it's not a good idea for anyone to connect their complete identity with a company or a particular job; self-worth is attained when a good balance between work and personal life is maintained.

## Examine Reward Systems

It was clear in my interviews that these leaders understand the power of reward systems. They designed reward systems to reward desired behavior. This is often not the case. In the classic article, "On the Folly of Rewarding A While Hoping for B" in the *Academy of Management Executive* (1995), Steven Kerr describes how many reward systems are dysfunctional. He outlines the differences:

| We hope for ... | But we often reward ... |
| --- | --- |
| Long-term growth | Quarterly earnings |
| Teamwork | Individual effort |
| Setting "stretch" goals | Achieving goals to "make the numbers" |
| Commitment to quality | Shipping on time even with defects |
| Candor and honesty | Reporting good news, agreeing with the boss |

Source: Adapted from Kerr, S. (1995), p. 12

Kerr first wrote the article in 1975 and it was reprinted in 1995 as a classic because things have not changed that much. In the article, he talks about how in medicine, we treat illness instead of rewarding wellness. In higher education, we want excellent teachers, but we still reward research. Since people behave in ways that are rewarded, leaders need to examine reward systems to make sure they are rewarding behaviors that they desire.

One of the strong themes among these companies was how they included rewards to reinforce work-life integration (balance). As Fasha Mahjoor, Founder and President of Phenomenex, a global chemical specialty company in California as well as other parts of the world, told me, "If you don't create a work-life balance, how do employees stay in the game—showing up every day, succeeding and exceeding expectations? We have to create an environment that is worthy of their presence." He continued to describe how they have been known to bring in a high school marching band to march through the buildings when they have something to celebrate. "We are not creating this culture for PR and publicity. We don't relish the idea of talking about culture. We are doing these things because they resonate with people. We have an environment of arts and antiques and people are having fun."

It was common to hear leaders talk about on-site health facilities that include yoga instructors and quiet rooms for meditation. Paid days off are often allocated for employees to give back to the community and volunteer. I was told how leaders were awarding people with so many "wellness days" instead of "sick days." If people were not ill, they were rewarded with paid days off for being well. This is an example of a functional reward system and rewarding desired behaviors.

## Connection to Higher Purpose

As noted earlier in this book, leaders who connect with empathy and compassion are in a good position to help their employees deal with emotional and spiritual damage in times when jobs seem to come and go like the wind. This leadership sometimes even includes making a spiritual leader available to each employee.

Tyson Foods Inc. and Vermeer Corporation are among a growing pool of companies that allocate funds to have a corporate chaplain on call. Vermeer's company chaplain is on contract full time with Workplace and Family Life Services, Vermeer's employee assistance program. At the time of my interview, the chaplain was a United Methodist pastor and a certified military and corporate chaplain. He described his position to me as "standing beside people in times of crisis, and walking through these times with them to provide support and encouragement." These companies understand that providing these services is an investment that is returned in outcomes such as productivity, satisfaction, and employee well-being.

After interviewing Ann Coombs, author of *The Living Workplace: Soul, Spirit, and Success in the 21st Century,* I discovered a framework and audit for helping leaders create a living workplace called SWOT. For many of us, this is an acronym recognized as Strengths, Weaknesses, Opportunities, and Threats. Coombs has put an interesting twist on the typical SWOT analysis. In this framework, the letters stand for Spirit, Wisdom, Openness, and Thoughtfulness. This opens up a conversation about how to knit these qualities into the fabric of workplaces.

Coombs has created an audit to be used internally with employees to determine how well the organization measures up to expectations in these areas. Coombs told me how the typical SWOT analysis is an aggressive term, and she wanted to change the language in the workplace to change how people think, talk, and act—so they will live differently in workplaces. The SWOT analysis is one of the exercises in the Workshop Suggestions section at the end of this chapter.

Nicholas Piramal India, Ltd., a pharmaceuticals manufacturing and research organization, is another organization that has incorporated spiritual values into their management approach. In fact, the CEO uses his self-published book called *The Light Has Come to Me* to guide the company's management philosophy. The company provides the opportunity for spiritual connection to all employees by allowing employees of all religions to express their own spiritual beliefs (including a support for yoga and meditation) in their daily work life. Employees can even request a "Spiritual Day" in addition to regular vacation leave.

While this level of spiritual connection is somewhat unusual, many companies I interviewed (Eileen Fisher, Omega Institute, Hearthstone Homes, Phenomenex, Tomasso) offer opportunities for employee introspection by providing facilities such as a "quiet room" for reflection, mediation, or prayer. The decision to provide these employee services reflects not only enlightened leadership practices, but also good business practice with positive customer impact.

Jerry Broccolo, Vice President of Spirituality at Catholic Health Initiatives, said his organization's practice of providing in-service retreats and days of reflection for leaders, staff, physicians, and board members affects how patients are treated. He stated:

> "We treat you as a human person, not as a medical condition. We provide person-centered care, not patient-centered care. We want a staff that consists of whole-person(s) caregiver engaging the whole-person patient. This mindset enables you to deliver excellent care. In this culture, the retention of nurses has increased because they find meaning, care, and compassion in their work. But this kind of culture requires a transformation of senior leaders who need to 'get it,' otherwise they are obstacles and the culture is not sustainable."

J.-Robert Ouimet, CEO of Tomasso, said that it is common practice to include a meal with the spouse or partner of a newly hired employee to demonstrate the importance of family. Ouimet told me that this intimate connection solidifies his notion that "Kindness is a language we all can speak." The importance of connection and human dignity is also emphasized through special awards given to those who exhibit valued practices such as listening.

Tomasso supports "inner listening" as well by providing employee quiet rooms and moments of silence at the start of each meeting. "We need to reach our hearts through silence in order to listen to the inner voice. We need to get quiet in order to hear and to get rid of the noise in our head."

Even with the sense of community built by the organization, Tomasso is still a business that responds to market conditions, and this sometimes includes letting employees go. Managers are required to have two face-to-face meetings with the employee and to use a process called "nurturing out" that emphasizes human dignity and humility. Ouimet explained, "We use a process called 'nurturing out,' if that is appropriate. Basically, the focus is on explaining how it may not be a good fit if the person is not performing up to expectation. There must be a reason and we try to protect human dignity and communicate these decisions guided by humility."

Since learning about "nurturing out," I have shared this concept in workshops, in writings, and with friends in leadership positions. As Edward Deming, the continuous quality improvement guru, liked to say, "Most people are not bad employees, but they are stuck in bad systems." Deming advocated that most people want to do a good job. When they don't, it is probably because the system is bad or not a good "fit." There is probably a reason why they are not performing well. Having honest conversations with them should help them realize they should seek a place where they can perform and where their talents can be utilized and valued.

Peter Roy, former President and COO of Whole Foods, reinforced Ouimet's conclusions in my conversations with him:

> "It is challenging to practice servant leadership in these times. Leaders have to make hard decisions, but it is how decisions are carried out and communicated that is important. With intention, we can do that with empathy and caring. How people are treated on the way out impacts the people who remain. Leaders who resist laying off people if needed, do a disservice to everyone else. Caring does not mean avoiding tough choices."

At Eileen Fisher, Inc., Susan Shors told me how employees are allocated $1,000 to spend on wellness and the same amount to spend on education. Employees are reimbursed for self-care activities such as yoga, facials, gym memberships, dance lessons, voice lessons, educational classes or seminars, or any other way in which the employee wishes to learn. In addition, Eileen Fisher offers an in-house yoga program and other benefits, such as a discussion group for parents with young children facilitated by a qualified psychologist. People are held accountable for how they used the money in their Professional Development Plans. This system rewards the health and well-being of employees with the understanding that their wellness improves productivity and satisfaction.

## The Power of Storytelling

If you want to change the culture, change the stories that you tell. Most people would prefer a story over a lecture and we can remember stories. Nightime Pediatrics Clinics is a Salt Lake City business that operates several after-hours clinics in the area. Teresa Lever-Pollary, company CEO, said that one of her roles is to "solidify culture so it extends beyond the president and me" (Stewart, 1998, 165). In this case, she brought together positive stories of how all the stakeholders in the success of the clinic treated each other, including patients, doctors, nurses, administrative staff and others. The self-published book is a powerful narrative for the positive impact of treating everyone with dignity and respect.

Christina Baldwin, author of *Storycatching* (2005) and *The Circle Way* (2010), describes how leaders should be architects in structuring conversations to be more effective and meaningful. According to Baldwin, there are four universal laws of respect that are articulated as circle agreements:

- We will hold stories or personal material in confidentiality.
- We listen to each other with compassion and curiosity.
- We ask for what we need and offer what we can.
- We agree to employ a group guardian to watch our need, timing, and energy. We agree to pause at a signal, and to call for that signal when we feel the need to pause.

Baldwin said the main benefit of using the circle to share stories and build community is that people feel safe when they know each other better. She said, "We need to know each other's story in order to care about them." She used the example of how people fill up their cubicles and offices with their "stories" (photos, mementos, plaques) so that we might ask about them. When we ask them to explain the significance, we find connections and threads of commonality among us. "People tell stories all the time, but who is listening? We need to stop and listen."

## Physical Connections

Of course, quiet rooms are not the only way to connect with our inner and outer selves. Toyota Motor Sales, USA, Inc. in Torrance, California is at the experiential edge of education and personal development. This organization takes a different approach aimed at developing its employees' capacity and appreciation for high-performance teamwork and cooperation through the use of drumming at University of Toyota's Drum Circle. This alternative approach to other experiential team-building adventures, such as obstacle courses, wall climbing, and other forms of physical challenges, helps participants develop better ways to cooperate, resolve challenges or conflicts, and work through problems. It's also a great deal of fun.

Creating a workplace that encourages employee engagement, satisfaction, and productivity takes intention, thoughtfulness, and commitment. The senior leaders I interviewed stressed that when employees are comfortable bringing their mind, body, and spirit to work they are more intrinsically motived. The meaning they find in their work is more valuable than money or any other form of reward.

### Workshop Suggestions

1. **Create a Culture Book**

   *Description:* The purpose of this exercise is to have teams from organizations create a book based on individual stories and experiences that resulted from just being in the organization.

*Instructions:* In these days of self-publishing, it is easy to create a book of stories that can be shared as a way of preserving or changing the culture. Employees submit stories and an editorial panel can select. Share the stories in all kinds of settings, such as the opening of a meeting or with prospective employees.

2.  **The SWOT Framework (Spirit, Wisdom, Openness, Thoughtfulness)**

    *Description:* This exercise involves conducting an audit to assess how well people in the organization are experiencing respect, dignity, honor, honesty, acceptance, appreciation, truth, love, and integrity—characteristics of a supportive workplace.

    *Instructions:* This audit comes from the book *The Living Workplace: Soul, Spirit, and Success in the 21st Century* (2004) by Ann Coombs. She developed a framework to determine if the qualities of spirit, wisdom, openness, and thoughtfulness are knitted into the fabric of the organization. You can refer to her book for the complete audit and create a similar framework for employees to complete. Employees assess the organization on spirit, wisdom, openness, and thoughtfulness by rating statements on a scale to what extent they perceive the statement to be true (consistently, often, sometimes, and rarely). If the goal is to create a healthy workplace, then it is important to assess how well the goal is being met. Note that the audit is much broader than employee satisfaction that is typically measured. Culture includes more than satisfying employees.

    Examples of characteristics for SWOT:
    **Spirit:**
    • is committed to speaking and acting upon the truth

- believes in the people he or she manages or supervises

- believes in the purpose of the organization or business

- supports people in and through their work.

**Wisdom:**

- sees what is really going on

- acts with clarity and purpose

- knows what is right, not just what works

- understands how and why people thrive and grow in the workplace.

**Openness:**

- communicates clearly and concisely

- gives honest, respectful answers

- asks direct, genuine questions

- gives feedback that enhances and supports professional and personal development of the other person.

**Thoughtfulness:**

- cares for people in your organization

- is compassionate without ignoring accountability issues

- cares about how the little pieces fit into the big picture

- takes time and makes space to think and to reflect.

3. **Ask Employees Questions**

*Description:* The purpose of this exercise is to ask questions to find out what people honestly think and how they feel about working for the organization.

*Instructions:* In a nonthreatening manner, ask employees questions such as: What would make a meaningful workplace? How do you feel about the culture? Do you feel you can speak honestly and be heard? Create a large collective mural or make individual drawings that reflect how people feel about the culture. Share these stories as a way of creating a broader and ongoing conversation about culture.

### 4. Create a Drum Circle

*Description:* The purpose is to create a circle where people participate in a rhythm.

*Instructions:* Arrange people in a circle and make "instruments" available that can be beat on as a drum or can be shaken to a common rhythm. Anything that can be used as "drumsticks" or as shakers can be used (such as jars with rocks, spatulas, steel spoons, plastic eggs with candy inside). Start a beat and have people follow—changing the beat at times. Then select various people to "solo" while the rest of the group continues the beat. This exercise illustrates concepts such as leading, following, and listening. I usually ask people how they felt during the exercise, since it can be used to reduce stress.

### 5. Examine Reward Systems

*Description:* The purpose of this exercise is to intentionally examine organizational reward systems to determine the behaviors that are being rewarded.

*Instructions:* People behave in ways that are rewarded. The organizational culture influences people's thoughts, behaviors, and actions. It is essential to understand what behaviors are being rewarded. Most reward systems are dysfunctional and can be changed when critically examined to reward desired behaviors.

## Readings

Zappos, the world's largest online shoe store, publishes a book about their organization's culture every year. I highly recommend ordering the book and using it as a model. I also suggest reading *The Corner Office: Indispensable and Unexpected Lessons from CEOs on How to Lead and Succeed* by Adam Bryant. This book is a compilation of interviews with CEOs and senior leaders about the cultures they are trying to create. Every week in the Sunday Business section of the *New York Times,* Bryant continues to interview CEOs probing them for specifics about their hiring practices and how they are creating cultures where people want to work. He recognizes that with each person hired, the organizational culture is influenced—either in good ways or bad.

A classic article I use for discussing reward systems is "On the Folly of Rewarding A While Hoping for B" (1995) by Steven Kerr. People behave in ways that are rewarded, so it is important to examine reward systems—particularly since many reward, systems are dysfunctional. This article does an excellent job of bringing to our attention to how reward systems influence the culture—positively and negatively.

In addition, there are several excellent online sources (webinars, YouTube, podcasts) that provide creative ideas about how leaders are designing interesting cultures in these uncertain times. If you do a search on YouTube, you can find some of the most prominent senior leaders and leadership authors talking about how they build a healthy culture. Daniel Pink has a radio show called *Office Hours* where about once a month he interviews a special guest about work, business, and life. He compares this show to *Car Talk* for the human engine. You can subscribe to the podcasts at www.danielpink.com.

Judi Neal, chairman of Edgewalkers International and one of my sages, conducts a teleconference series where she interviews leaders about how they are creating holistic cultures. TEDTalks (www.ted.com) are another good way to listen to "ideas worth sharing." There is even a TEDWomen series focused on "women reshaping the future." Google brings in key thought leaders and authors during their "authors@ google" lunch and learns. Listening to some of these sources of current information remind us that a key part of our legacy should be on creating a culture where people want to work.

## What's Next?

Leaders create their legacy every day through the decisions they make, how they make them, and the way those impacted are treated along the way. This chapter discusses the concept of "living legacy" and the transformational potential of approaching leadership in this holistic way.

# Chapter 9

# Leaders Live Their Legacy

*The legacy we leave is based on the life we lead.*

*—Jim Kouzes*

*Life is a progression of development and wisdom that comes*

*from learning from life experiences.*

*—Richard Leider*

M ost leaders start thinking about their legacy at the end of their careers. But what exactly does the term legacy mean and how should leaders think about this important responsibility?

When I ask the leaders who attend my workshop and classes about their perception of legacy, many associate the concept with what others believe or say about us when we retire or die. While that is true for most of us, leaders have a special responsibility to be aware of the legacy they are creating every day and make their decisions accordingly. It's an important concept for leaders, because leaders who live the legacy they want to create focus on and make decisions based on what matters most. And perhaps most importantly, a focus on legacy helps leaders pass along real wisdom gained through the digested lessons of life experience.

If you start thinking about it now, you will increase the odds of leaving a legacy that reflects your best qualities, as well as elements of your leadership you would like to see embedded in the fabric of the organization. Your leadership legacy is the sum total of the difference you make in people's lives, directly and indirectly, formally and informally. The way you behave in your day-to-day life defines your legacy. The challenge is how to live in a way that creates a legacy others want to be a part of too—that others want to follow.

## Legacy Thinking

Your legacy is built moment by moment, in small interactions. How you live your legacy can uplift people's spirits and inspire them to live or perform better than they thought possible. Or it can drag them down and create the opposite effect. As defined by Robert Galford and Regina Maruca (2006) in *Your Leadership Legacy: Why Looking Toward the Future Will Make You a Better Leader Today*, "Legacy thinking is a tool through which leaders can filter and assess their decisions … It also serves as a powerful check to help leaders ensure that their priorities—personal and organizational—are reflected in their actions."

Since organizational success can come at a personal price, future leaders need to realize the impact they are having on others and do this on a regular and ideally daily basis. Cameron (2012), Lawrence and Nohria (2002), and Covey (2004) are a few of the authors who believe a basic human need or drive is to create a legacy. They recognize the significance of leaders having a long-term impact through their work—that their influence extends beyond them.

Richard Leider, author of *The Power of Purpose* (2012) and an executive coach, told me that the process of building this critical leadership capacity is a spiritual evolution based on the development of truth we've gathered, studied, and stored. He said we gain knowledge through our experiences, but gain wisdom by learning how to see the big picture and knowing how to determine what is important.

To help leaders understand this critical skill, Leider takes groups of senior executives to Africa to learn how tribes value their elders and the wisdom they possess. He said, "In Africa, elders have seen and lived through many events and they are the wisdom people—the only source for true wisdom. Today, we mistake information for wisdom. In fact, we are drowning in information and starving for wisdom. We know the wise ones when we are around them. We can tell when we are in their presence."

# The Elders

The Elders (www.theelders.org) is a great example of wisdom at work in the world. Nelson Mandela, Mary Robinson, and Jimmy Carter are members. According to Richard Leider, elders can "hold the larger space in order to engage other people in dialogue. Elders can rise above the government and look at what is best for the whole because they no longer have a political stake in the world, but rather a spiritual stake."

Organizational and management legend Peter Senge was another sage who noted the importance of celebrating and learning from the wisdom of experience. "There is a difference between getting older and becoming a sage," he told me one day as he was commuting to his office at MIT in Boston. "It is the process of reflecting on life's experience that leads to sage-like wisdom. Although age provides more experience of coping with adversity, just getting older does not guarantee wisdom." Warren Bennis said it this way, "Judgment doesn't happen in a blink. It accumulates over time and not in a flash. Intuition is the opportunity to reflect on knowledge."

This legacy of wisdom has been part of Native American culture for many generations and is embodied in a tradition called the "Seventh Generation." According to the practice, decisions are made based on how the decision will affect the seventh generation that comes after the decision is made. Many organizations and their leaders seem to be using an opposite form of decision making today—choosing short-term gain over long-term benefit and legacy. As Angeles Arrien told me, "There's a place in leadership where you have to align with wisdom in order to be truly effective. The choices that we make from places of power are different from the decisions we make from places of wisdom."

Daniel Seymour, a recognized higher education administrator and author, said that he developed a mantra over the years based on his life experience. As a leader, he tells his team: Be smart. Be kind. Be brave. He said that if you say the mantra over and over again, people will believe you. "Developing a worldview is like sharpening a dull pencil over the years. It is grounded theory. Life experience gives you more examples to confirm or not confirm your theory. My worldview is shaped from all of my life experiences."

Living a legacy is the last chapter of this book because it is the capstone to the other chapters. Leaders who are self-aware, demonstrate compassion, stay connected, are willing to be vulnerable, model resilience, and create places where people want to work are living a legacy because they are positively influencing the lives of other people. Leaders who lead in this intentional way are also modeling "legacy thinking."

It can be helpful to look for people who are living a life that you want to lead. When Tim Russert died suddenly, I was struck by how he was remembered by the media. Based on the eulogies shared, he was someone who was living his legacy daily (see the sidebar).

## Leader as Sage

When Tim Russert died unexpectedly, I listened to the words and phrases used to describe him. People did not use the word "boss," but they described how they had lost their leader, mentor, supporter, friend, colleague, teacher. Betsy Fischer, Russert's executive assistant for several years, said that Tim's favorite form of exercise was "bending over to lift someone up."

Common words and phrases for describing Russert included:

- honest and with the highest integrity
- tough but fair
- generous with his time and sharing his expertise
- joy in his work and in his relationships
- authentic—the most authentic, according to Tom Brokow
- never lost his roots
- transparent

- knew who he was and never forgot it

- listened to everyone.

And the list went on.

As one commentator said, "It is easy to say these nice things about a person after they are gone. The difference here is that the words about Tim are all true." Peggy Noonan wrote an editorial in the *Wall Street Journal* (June 21-22, 2008) titled "A Life's Lesson." While some people started to complain that the coverage had gone on too long, Noonan reminded us that it was a beautiful tribute. "The media for four days told you the keys to a life well lived, the things you actually need to live life well, and without which it won't be as good." Among them:

- "Taking care of those you love and letting them know they're loved; which involves self-sacrifice."

- "Holding firm to God, to your religious faith, no matter how high you rise or low you fall. This involves guts, self-discipline, and active attention to developing and refining a conscience to whose promptings you can respond."

- "Honoring your calling or profession by trying to do it within honorable work, which takes effort and a willingness to master the ethics of your field."

- "And enjoying life."

Michael Gartner told another story that illustrates the character of Tim Russert. Gartner was the president of NBC News who was instrumental in Russert's becoming the moderator of *Meet the Press*. Gartner's son, Christopher, idolized Russert. When Christopher died in 1994 at age 17 from an initial attack of juvenile diabetes, it was the phone call from Russert that Gartner remembers well. He had left

NBC by then, but within hours of Christopher's death, the phone rang and it was Russert. In the words of Gartner:

"I was in tears and he seemed to be, too. He expressed his deep sorrow and then he said: 'Look, if God had come to you 17 years ago and said, *I'll make you a bargain. I'll give you a beautiful, wonderful, happy, and healthy kid for 17 years and then I'll take him away,* you would have made that deal in a second.'

He was right, of course, that was the deal. I just didn't know it. As it turns out, there was a similar deal—the terms were 58 years—with Tim. We just didn't know it. But we—his family, his friends, his guests, and his viewers, all of us so enriched by him—would have made it in a second."

---

## Ways to Live Your Legacy

The power of storytelling has always been part of my workshops and classes, but today's organizations and their leaders cannot afford to ignore the benefits of engaging their workforce through storytelling. Why? Because stories stick with people; and because of a simple truth that if you want to change the culture, you must change the stories that you tell.

Stories help organizations integrate new members, explain why the organization exists, and emphasize what values are important. Stories play a critical role in institutional memory—and stories are the principal means by which memories and wisdom are passed on through time.

## Sharing Life Stories

Howard Behar told me organizations should make a habit of using stories to demonstrate how their leaders do the right things for the right reasons. After all, most of us like to tell stories that explain our struggles and concerns. For the most part, we're interested in listening to the stories of others. Stories, as pointed out in chapter 6, help leaders build a sense of community and share wisdom with those they lead.

According to Dan and Chip Heath, authors of *Made to Stick* (2007), stories are effective teaching tools because they make the information "sticky." Craig Newmark (www.Craigslist.com) reports that some people read his website's lists "just for the personal stories." Telling and listening to stories creates empathy and helps those in organizations find common ground. The practice of conducting meetings in a circle, noted in chapter 8, is an example of small changes to traditional practices that encourage storytelling. The bottom line is that whether we are "claiming our place at the fire" as an elder in the organization, building a sense of community, or simply telling our story, finding ways to share our life experiences is how we pass on wisdom and these stories become part of a leadership legacy people remember.

StoryCorps (www.storycorps.org)—the largest oral history project in the nations' history—is based on the understanding that the telling of stories is one of the best ways of expressing the wisdom among people or from one generation to the next. StoryCorps broadcasts weekly on National Public Radio's *Morning Edition* and its popularity underscores the idea that everyone has an important story to tell. Some of the most remarkable stories were published in a book titled *Listening Is an Act of Love* by Dave Isay (2007). More than 50,000 people have shared their stories since 2003 and all the stories and conversations are preserved at the Library of Congress. Dave Isay, the founder of StoryCorps, says, "By listening closely to one another, we can help illuminate the true character of this nation, reminding us all just how precious each day can be and how truly great it is to be alive."

When I asked Peter Senge what had influenced his thinking about leadership, he offered Bill O'Brien, former CEO of Hanover Insurance, as an example. Senge described how at the end of every year, O'Brien wrote extensively about each year's journey and the lessons he had learned. "Few managers write as part of their management practice. It was a practical quest for him to be a better leader." And once written, O'Brien's efforts at telling his story became part of his legacy and the sharing of wisdom.

Erik Erikson, best known for his work in human development, in particular his Eight Stages of Psychosocial Development, used the term "generativity" to discuss the need in midlife for adults to begin telling stories that reflect on what they have learned. Often, these adults start to think about the impact they are making on others, instead of focusing on climbing the corporate ladder. Suddenly, these individuals are awakened to consider those who helped them succeed and to the need "to give something back."

Erickson captured the concept of generativity in the phrase "I am what survives me." John Korte called it "outliving the self." As adults move into and through midlife, they may become especially cognizant of their own mortality, and they may come to ponder how their lives may eventually end and what legacies they will leave behind. If that generativity is aimed toward future generations, it is natural that people's anticipations of their own life endings should be informed by their sense of generativity.

"The narrative beauty of generativity is that it provides a way of thinking about the end of one's life that suggests that the end is not really the end. I may die, but my children will live on. My own story may end, but other stories will follow mine, due in part to my own generative efforts" (Freedman, 2011, 96). John Gardner in his book *On Leadership*, said it this way, "If one is leading, teaching, dealing with young people or engaged in any other activity that involves influencing, directing, guiding, helping, or nurturing, the whole tone of the relationship is conditioned by one's faith in human possibilities. That is the generative element, the source of the current that gives life to the relationship" (66).

Considering your impact on the world earlier in your career rather than later is a powerful concept and one supported in the work of Robert Galford and Regina Maruca, authors of *Your Leadership Legacy* (2006). "Thinking about your legacy now makes you a better leader today no matter how far you are from retirement," the authors advocate. Likewise, Jim Kouzes and Barry Posner state in *A Leader's Legacy* (2006) that thinking about legacy encourages us to think about today's actions in a larger context. Legacy thinking requires us to go beyond the common practice of short-term thinking because legacies include the past, present, and future.

As leaders, whether you realize it or not, you are leaving a legacy with every decision or action you take. Your legacy is revealed in how others who work with you feel and think about you. Think of your legacy as a photomosaic: an image made up of any other tiny images. When you stand up close, you can see each image on its own as a single picture. But when viewed from a distance, all of the images together create a whole image that the artist wants you to see. Your leadership photomosaic is comprised of your approach to leadership, how you treat others, and what others think of your time as their leader.

## Mentoring

Another way of living your legacy is through the practice of mentoring. It can be an effective way to live your legacy as a leader. Not only does mentoring present a perfect opportunity to share your story with others, it allows you to pass along the wisdom you've gained through experience. But mentoring others or finding a mentor for yourself does not automatically happen.

Suku Radia, a CEO, makes an intentional effort to seek out younger people to mentor. He makes himself available at set times during the week or weekend to meet with people for informal conversations. He builds mentoring into his schedule and into his goals so that it happens.

Mentoring can also build intergenerational relationships that benefit not only the emerging leader, but the senior leader as well. Connie Wimer, CEO of Business Publications, Inc., told me, "I have always surrounded myself with older people. We can learn from their successes and from the mistakes of others. There is so much to learn from the life experiences of others." Wimer is now one of the most sought-out leaders in the community because people want to learn from her experiences.

Growing in wisdom involves continuing to learn. Younger people also have knowledge to share. Wisdom is based on processing life experience and this can be done and shared at any age. Engaging in mentoring relationships is one way to "walk the talk" of being generous and sharing what you know with others. It is rewarding to see others benefit from our life experience.

Fasha Mahjoor, Founder and President of Phenomenex, said it this way: "When you are 'living' your mission statement, that is the ultimate coaching—better than any consultant or coach. Our values are engrained in us and provide a vivacious energy that, in turn, energizes the people around us. When you are true to yourself and to your mission, people can relate to you."

Another way to view mentoring is to see yourself as a teacher. "Our own learning increases exponentially when we discuss what is meaningful for us with others, when we experience something personally that is invaluable, or when we teach what we have learned to someone else" (Arrien, 2011, 195-196). What do you know that you could teach others? How might you make an intentional effort to share what you know? As we pass on our wisdom to others, we are leaving our legacy. See the Workshop Suggestions at the end of this chapter for some effective mentoring suggestions.

## Creating an Ethical Will

Most of us are familiar with wills as legal documents that describe how we want to allocate our financial assets upon our death. We spend time and money making sure our assets are passed on according to our desires. But few of us take the time to document what is important to us in terms of beliefs and values—what matters most.

An ethical will is a document that outlines what you value as a leader now and how you'd like to see these values continued in your organization. While many people create these documents at turning points in their life—when they face challenging life situations or at transitional life stages—you can use the format to capture exactly what you believe so that these beliefs continue in your organization.

Values and worth are not determined by what we keep, but by what we give away. Being intentional about how we give away our beliefs and values is an important part of living our legacy. Excellent examples of ethical wills can be found at www.ethicalwills.com.

Similar to an ethical will is a legacy letter or statement. A legacy statement should be reviewed and updated as you gain additional life experiences. It isn't so much about making a statement as it is about a way of thinking. Legacy thinking is grounded in self-awareness, hopes, and intentions. It is focused on what we are leaving behind, wherever we go, whatever we do, and with whomever we encounter along the way. Legacy can be thought of as similar to the cliché, "Character is how you act when no one is looking." Because even if we don't think about the impact we are making, others are noticing, whether we like it or not.

Think of two people who are building meaningful legacies. How are they doing it? What decisions are they making? What behaviors are repeated? How do others respond to them? Conversely, avoid those whose behaviors you do not respect.

Richard Leider, author of several books including *The Power of Purpose: Creating Meaning in Your Life and Work, Claiming Your Place at the Fire*, and *The Second Half of Life*, interviewed more than 1,000 people who had distinguished careers with leading companies. He asked them to reflect upon what they had learned and what they would do differently if given the chance to start over. Some top themes that emerged include:

- Life picks up speed and the focus shifts as we move through our careers. We tend to think about our legacy and what we are leaving behind instead of how high we are climbing in later career stages.
- Taking time to be reflective is important, as well as not getting so caught up in the "doing" to the exclusion of "being" and "meaning."

- Risk-taking is part of creativity, learning, and growing and this exploring make us feel more alive.

- Doing something that contributes value beyond yourself provides fulfillment and purpose.

In many of my courses and workshops, I use the movie *About Schmidt* as an illustration of legacy. Warren Schmidt (Jack Nicholson) is unprepared for and depressed by his life after retirement. He has spent his entire life working at a job that could have been done by anybody, or nobody. Because he did not plan for life after retirement, he lives a life without purpose. The movie takes us on a journey of Warren trying to find himself. The bottom line is this: If you are what you do and you don't do it anymore, then who are you?

Because my neighbor was Jack Nicholson's body double in *About Schmidt* and he is a funny guy, I expected the movie to be a comedy. Instead, I left the movie feeling sad, but on a quest to live my future much differently than Warren Schmidt and to help others do the same. I have been on mission to retire the word "retirement," because life goes beyond work.

In fact, our life's work continues as long as we live and our legacy continues with it. Many people are starting "encore careers" or finding other ways of working that add value and meaning. These themes were reinforced on my unexpected journey of seeking wisdom and learning about leadership. Leadership legacies are built by each decision and action or inaction on a daily basis. Even in these times when decisions are difficult to make, we still have control over how we make them and how they are communicated. Jim Kouzes summarized it this way, "The legacy you leave is the life you lead. And leaders must decide what matters in life before they can live a life that matters."

We need to live our legacy daily by reflecting on the decisions we make, how we treat others, and how we live each day. The only time we have is now.

We need to find our calling and contribute to someone or someplace that will live beyond us. Perhaps Howard Behar said it best:

*"We need a purpose bigger than ourselves. There has to be a purpose larger than making money and a name for ourselves. Our purpose needs to be greater than the individual that supersedes all of us and serves society. My purpose is to nurture and inspire the human spirit. I start with myself and then work to do this with others. That's how I want to live my life and how I want to be remembered."*

## Workshop Suggestions

1.  **Personal Board of Directors**

    *Description:* The purpose of this exercise is to create a group of people whom you trust and from whom you can seek advice and counsel.

    *Instructions:* What kind of legacy are you living and how do you know? Select four to six people who care about you, want to see you succeed, and will give you honest feedback. These are people whom you contact when you need their perspective, advice, and wisdom. They hold you accountable and give you support. These are people who will help you minimize your blind spots (for example, they tell you when you have broccoli in your teeth!).

2.  **Leadership Learning Plan**

    *Description:* This exercise is to develop a plan that incorporates learning goals into leadership development.

*Instructions:* Develop a plan that includes the following components: 1) personal mission statement, 2) vision statement, 3) personal balance sheet of assets and liabilities (opportunities for improvement), 4) professional goals for the next three years and milestones for measurement and accountability, and 5) learning goals that will enrich your life.

### 3. This I Believe

*Description:* This exercise involves writing a leadership philosophy to guide how you lead.

*Instructions:* Use the prompt: "This I believe …" to write your leadership philosophy. This document can serve as your moral compass, keeping you on the right path. When your beliefs and actions are consistent with your values, then you are living your legacy.

## Personal Development Suggestions

### 1. Author Your Own Book About Yourself

*Description:* This exercise involves writing a book—a memoir or a collection of life experiences.

*Instructions:* With self-publishing as an affordable and available option, it is possible to leave your legacy by writing your own autobiography or memoir as a legacy. This can also be done by blogging about what matters most.

### 2. Write an Ethical Will or Legacy Letter

*Description:* This exercise involves documenting what values, beliefs, and commitments are important to you as a way of passing them on to others.

*Instructions:* An ethical will outlines what you value now and how to insure the continuation of those values for future generations. A legacy letter is another name for documenting what is most important to be shared with others. It can be written at any age since we don't know when our life will end. Examples of ethical wills can be found at www.ethicalwills.com.

Questions to ask when writing an ethical will or legacy letter:

- What are the lessons that you've learned in life?

- What are you most proud of?

- What are your biggest regrets?

- What are your spiritual beliefs?

- What will you miss most when you are gone?

- Who are the most important people in your life? What did you learn from them?

- If you only had a year left to live, what would you do?

- What are lessons learned from grandparents/parents/siblings/spouse/children?

- What are things or people for whom I am grateful?

- What are my hopes for the future?

### 3. Legacy Statement

*Description:* The purpose of this exercise is to write a legacy statement.

*Instructions:* A legacy statement goes beyond describing the actions or symbols of which you are most proud. Those things are for obituaries. Legacy statements focus more on the characteristics and values for which you would most like to be remembered.

Answer the following questions. Then use the responses to write a legacy statement that can be used to guide your actions and behaviors.

- How do you wish to be remembered as a leader by those inside and outside your organization, both in your current role and in your career? State two or three personal characteristics (skills, behaviors, or values) for which you would most like to be remembered. How would you like to have these characteristics manifest themselves? How would people know?

- What have you learned in your current role, your work, and your life so far that you would most like to pass onto others?

- How will you convey that learning?

- What else do you want to accomplish? Why is this important in building or completing your legacy?

- Besides more time, what will help or impede you in completing what remains to be accomplished?

Source: Adapted from Galford, R.M., and Maruca, R.F. (2006).<br>Your Leadership Legacy. Boston: Harvard Business School Publishing.

### 4. Find a Role Model

*Description:* This exercise is about intentionally seeking out a person who can be a role model—someone from whom you can learn.

*Instructions:* Focus on someone whom you would have followed in the past or would be happy to follow. Why would you follow them? We all know a good leader we would follow—living or not, man or woman or animal, mortal or immortal, real or mythic, even a character in a novel. How might we lead our life in a similar way?

### 5. Mentor Others

*Description:* This exercise is to share what you have learned with others.

*Instructions:* Be intentional about mentoring others. Make yourself available for informal conversations with emerging leaders. Build it into your schedule so that it happens. When you make it a priority, you learn that giving is better than receiving. And when you mentor or teach others, your legacy is being left with each person you influence.

## Readings

Two excellent books on legacy are *A Leader's Legacy* (2006) by Jim Kouzes and Barry Posner and *Your Leadership Legacy* (2006) by Robert Galford and Regina Maruca. *A Leader's Legacy* includes short stories to be shared that resonate with leaders at all levels. *Your Leadership Legacy* integrates exercises such as writing a legacy statement and philosophy.

In addition to the website www.ethicalwill.com, a very good source for ethical wills is the book by Jo Kline Cebuhar titled *So Grows the Tree—Creating an Ethical Will—The Legacy of Your Beliefs and Values, Life Lessons and Hopes for the Future* (2010). It is written as a workbook that can guide you personally or be used in workshops.

## What's Next?

To wrap up, I draw some of my own conclusions about the research. The process of writing this book changed my life. It was a journey that was much broader and more extensive than I dreamed. This section explains how the people I met, the books and articles I read, and the activities in which I engaged (as suggested by the sages), have enriched me personally and professionally.

# Chapter 10

## Final Thoughts

I set out in 2004 on a quest to learn more about how to better prepare leaders for the future. The initial study was called "In Search of Sages" and I ended up interviewing more than 100 sages. Most of them are authors and coaches, and several of them are the senior leaders of organizations recognized for allowing people to bring their whole selves to work. A few of them even started their own organizations so that they could create the kind of environment for others in which they personally wanted to work.

My journey involved reading almost everything recommended to me along the way. I attended specific workshops with some of the top thought leaders in the field. In addition, I became certified as a Sage-ing Leader,© Registered Corporate Coach,® and Change Management Consultant with The Genysys Group. When I learned something new, I tried to put it into practice. All of the research and related experience has changed my life.

The main lessons from my journey have formed the framework for this book. But I also made some specific conclusions at the end. In chapter 9, I suggest an exercise called "This I Believe" as a way to write a leadership philosophy to guide how you lead. After everything that I have experienced since 2004 in the research process that culminated with this book, this is what I believe:

- It's best to live from the inside out. Fulfillment comes from knowing your talents and values and living with integrity.

- Life is a circular process of self-renewal, growth, and discovery rather than a linear sequence of accomplishments.

- Life is a story with many chapters. Each chapter has a beginning, an end, and a transition to the next chapter.

- We don't resist change as much as we resist transition. Understanding the process of transition is critical in order to lead ourselves and to influence others.

- Understanding transition can lead to personal growth and renewal that benefits us and everyone around us, both personally and professionally.

- Acknowledging our fear of dying, embracing death, and understanding the grief process enables us to be healthier people for influencing others.

- Face time is better than Facebook.

- Legacy thinking should be daily thinking. When we think about how we want to be remembered, we are more likely to live the legacy we want to leave.

- And leadership development is really about personal development. To be a good leader, you need to be a good person.

Ray Anderson, founder and former chairman of Interface Incorporated, the world's largest manufacturer of modular carpet, had an epiphany about saving the environment and even wrote *Midcourse Correction* (1999) to influence other leaders. Anderson told me working toward sustainability and a "zero footprint" is what got him up in the morning. Anderson said that after a talk he had given to a sales force meeting on a Tuesday in 1996, he received a poem over email out of the blue, an original poem written by a participant in the meeting. "It was evidence that my message was getting through to at least one person."

# Tomorrow's Child

Without a name; an unseen face
And knowing not our time nor place
Tomorrow's child, though yet unborn,
I saw you first last Tuesday morn.
A wise friend introduced us two,
And through his shining point of view
I saw a day which you would see;
A day for you, and not for me.
Knowing you has changed my thinking,
For I never had an inkling
That perhaps the things I do
Might someday, somehow, threaten you.
Tomorrow's Child, my daughter-son,
I'm afraid I've just begun
To think of you and of your good,
Though always having known I should.
Begin I will to weigh the cost
Of what I squander; what is lost
If ever I forget that you
Will someday come to live here too.

Source: Poem by Glenn Thomas. Read by Ray Anderson in a speech, "A Call for Systemic Change" presented at the Plenary Lecture at the 3rd National Conference on Science Policy and the Environment: "Education for a Sustainable and Secure Future." Sponsored by the National Council for Science and the Environment. January 31, 2003 in Washington, D.C.

Anderson said the poem "Tomorrow's Child" speaks to us across the generations with a simple, but profound message: "We are all part of the web of life. During our brief visit here, we have a choice to make: We can either help it or hurt it. The old mindset or the new? Exploitation and destruction, or restoration? Which will it be? Every day of your life with every action you take, every investment you make, everything you buy and every student you teach—it's your call."

The fact that Anderson wanted to share this poem, reflects that he was awake and willing to demonstrate his vulnerability. He knew that leaders from all kinds of organizations in a variety of industries were taking actions that were destroying the earth and he grieved for these losses. He did everything in his power to lead his organization with minimum damage to our natural resources. He was adamant that industries must change their ways in order to leave a "zero footprint."

After interviewing him and reading his book, I was convinced he was creating a place where people want to work. And he was proud of the fact that this was a critical part of his legacy. Anderson is being called the "greenest CEO in America." Another reflection of how important he was to the company is the fact that on their website (www.interfaceglobal.com) there is a blog dedicated to remembering their chairman and founder who died in August 2011. To remember the legacy of Ray, years later there is still a link dedicated to their adored chairman and founder that includes a video of the entire memorial service. What a sage!

As I said at the beginning of the book, I did not set out to write a book. In fact, when I started the interviews, I did not envision everything involved in this research. But I was so fascinated with what I was learning that I kept on going. Connie Wimer, chairman of Business

Publications, said this when I asked her about defining moments in her leadership journey: "There have not been any real defining moments, but it has been a million baby steps." What began as a quest to learn as much as I could about effective leadership, resulted in discovering unexpected wisdom from an unexpected journey. And in the end, I learned as much about life as I did about how to be a successful leader.

In closing, Brene Brown's book, *Daring Greatly: How the Courage to Be Vulnerable Transforms the Way We Live, Love, Parent, and Lead* (2013) and her TED talk on vulnerability was based on research that reinforced what I learned from the sages:

> "And so these folks had, very simply, the courage to be imperfect. They had the compassion to be kind to themselves first, and then to others, because, as it turns out, we can't practice compassion with other people if we can't treat ourselves kindly. And the last was they had connection, and—this was the hard part—as a result of authenticity, they were willing to let go of who they thought they should be, in order to be who they were, which you have to absolutely do that for connection."

As I reflect upon my sage interviews, I know there was something "different" and great about these people. They were so willing to share their wisdom with me, knowing that I was writing a book in order to pass it on to others. They had a kindred spirit, were generous with their time, and grateful for the chance to extend their legacy. When I was surprised to learn that Dr. Elmer Burack, one of my sages (and my main professional mentor), was undergoing cancer treatment, he said "This is one of the speed bumps that we expect at our age. While it may slow me down, it will not stop me from living." In fact, this book is dedicated to the memory of Elmer. Without Elmer's guidance and coaching, I would never have embarked on this wonderful learning journey.

Thank you to all of the sages in my study. I am grateful for the time you spent sharing your wisdom with me so that I could engage in this journey and share it with others. You have touched me and I have grown.

Becoming a sage is a journey and it takes a lifetime, but it is worth it. The goal is to make the rest of life the best of life. But we need to keep walking in order to make our own path. When we do this, we can share what we have learned with others. The fact that you are reading this book indicates you are interested in making the journey. The Spanish poet Antonio Machado reminds us that there are no answers. We just need to keep seeking—the path is made by walking.

*"Caminante, no hay camino. El camino se hace al andar."*
*Walker, there is no path. The path is made by walking.*

—Antonio Machado

Original photograph by Jann Freed.

# Appendix A

## Research Method and Knowledge Base

B eginning in 2004, the first phase of my research involved interviewing more than 100 authorities in the field of leadership, rang-
ing from Russ Ackoff to Peter Block, Max De Pree to Sally Helgesen, to
Margaret Wheatley. I also interviewed senior leaders in organizations
that received an award for being deeply committed to nurturing the
human spirit. My subjects included active and former CEOs, academ-
ics, leadership authors and consultants, and executive coaches (see Appendix B for the complete list). I particularly focused on leaders who
support creating a workplace where people are encouraged to bring
their whole selves to work—their mind, body, and spirit.

The interviewees for the most part support the principles consistent with servant leadership. According to Robert Greenleaf (2002),
the great leader is seen as a servant first. "One does not awaken each
morning with the compulsion to reinvent the wheel. But if one is a
servant, either leader or follower, one is always searching, listening,
expecting that a better wheel for these times is in the making. It may
emerge any day" (23). Based on my literature review, that is the type
of leadership being advocated and practiced by enlightened leaders in
these uncertain times.

# Method

The first phases of the study involved sending email messages with a one-page attachment explaining the study to 12 highly recognized authors and thought leaders in the field of leadership. They were asked if they would be willing to participate in a 30-minute telephone interview. Using what sociologists call a snowball method of sampling (Glaser and Strauss, 1985; Lincoln and Guba, 1985; Lawrence-Lightfoot, 2009), I searched for thought leaders to explore how best to prepare people to be the kinds of leaders needed in these difficult times.

The snowball method consists of asking each interviewee to recommend others whom they thought should be included in the project. One of the benefits of this sampling method is the access to difficult to reach populations. People who might not have agreed to participate were able to be included because they had been referred by someone they know personally. Over the course of nine years, the list continued to grow as a result of each interview. By the nature of this method, samples are usually not random or representative and could result in some bias. This phase provided rich background information.

Almost all of the interviewees are authors and have the expertise and experience that enables them to teach, coach, and lead others. Therefore, it was difficult to classify them into specific categories. A total of 101 people were interviewed, a mixture of academicians, executive coaches, and former and current CEOs or senior leaders (see Appendix B). The executive coaches focus on helping people find meaning in their life and work. Many of these coaches have been identified by the *Wall Street Journal* and *Forbes* as some of the top executive coaches in the country.

Five broad questions were asked of these interviewees:

- What do you consider to be the most significant works (books, articles) in the area of leadership and/or spirituality?

- What is your current thinking on the topics covered by these books/articles?

- How should management education be changed to be more effective for preparing people for the changing workplace?

- What significant question are you currently pondering?

- What questions would you have liked me to ask or is there anything else you want me to know?

Based on the responses to the first question about reference materials, I proceeded to read almost everything that was mentioned. To save time, interviewees often recommended that I read aspects of their own work that answered my questions. Therefore, I tried to read as much of their work as possible, at least focusing on the most recent.

The responses to question three, about preparing people to be the kinds of leaders needed in the future, led me to personally partake in these activities. These experiences are described throughout the book. I tried to follow their guidance as much as possible to prepare myself to be the kind of leader being advocated by these sages.

Simultaneously, I also interviewed organizational leaders and leadership authors for the International Center for Spirit at Work (ICSW) teleconference series founded by Judi Neal during a five-year period. This phase of the research study included interviewing senior leaders at 13 of the organizations that have received the International Spirit at Work Award (ISAW) by the ICSW. These awards are a way to recognize and reward organizations deeply committed to nurturing the human spirit and an opportunity for these leading-edge organizations to tell their stories and to be a model for other organizations interested in learning more about how others are breaking ground in this exciting new field.

Contact people were identified in the award literature. One person (sometimes two from each organization) was interviewed to gain specific information about how to create a meaningful workplace. Since Chief Executive Officers (CEOs) are responsible for setting the tone of the culture, the CEO was often the contact person for the organization. In addition to interviews, several documents were analyzed to provide more details about how these organizations are creating a meaningful workplace, such as the award application that usually included vision and mission statements, and numerous examples to address the award criteria.

The sample included 10 companies in the United States, and one company each in Germany, Australia, and India. For a list of the specific companies, see the table below.

| International Spirit at Work Award Recipients Interviewed | | |
|---|---|---|
| Clean ServicePower | Germany | 2006 |
| In Search of Common Ground | United States | 2006 |
| Jesuit Social Services | Australia | 2006 |
| Nicholas Piramal | India | 2006 |
| Catholic Health Initiatives | United States | 2005 |
| Ascension Health | United States | 2004 |
| Hearthstone Homes | United States | 2004 |
| PeaceHealth | United States | 2004 |
| Phenomenex | United States | 2004 |

| | | |
|---|---|---|
| Memorial Hermann Healthcare System | United States | 2003 |
| Sounds True, Inc. | United States | 2003 |
| Eileen Fisher, Inc. | United States | 2003 |
| Medtronics | United States | 2003 |

Six broad questions were asked of the senior leaders from organizations that received the International Spirit at Work Award:

- How long has your organization been on this journey of creating a place where the human spirit is nurtured?

- What were the driving forces for making this change?

- What specific examples illustrate how your organization nurtures the human spirit?

- What major changes took place and continue to take place in order to support this change in culture?

- What have been the benefits/challenges from engaging on this journey?

- What else should I have asked in order to understand how to integrate and support spirituality in the workplace?

In addition to asking these questions, the interviewee was asked to share any written information (such as an ASAW application, mission and vision statements, values) that included specific illustrations of spirit in the workplace or any evidence of positive outcomes to provide a more complete picture of the efforts involved in creating this organizational culture.

All interviews were conducted over the telephone and recorded. Extensive notes were also taken as a backup to the recordings. The interviews lasted on average 45 to 60 minutes and the interviews were transcribed to provide a written record. Data were gathered until there was a saturation point of repeated themes. Data were analyzed using the constant comparative method for discovering theory from data (Glaser and Strauss 1967; Lincoln and Guba 1985). This method consists of the following: first, data are unitized (the smallest pieces of information that can be understood in the context of the study are identified); then the units are categorized; and finally the patterns present in the categories are determined.

Interestingly, almost all of the interviewees stated that they did not consider themselves to be sages. But humility is a common virtue emphasized in many spiritual traditions and is a primary characteristic of a sage. Yet, being humble often contradicts many popular leadership models advocating charisma and so-called strong leadership. Jim Collins (2001) found that ego often gets in the way of effective leadership. The high response rate and the fact that few people declined to be interviewed reinforced my conclusion that most of these people were sages. Sharing what one has learned and giving back are sage behaviors that are taken seriously.

Most of the time, I was in awe after the interviews because of the kindness, generosity, and insights reflected during them. I felt as if I was in a sacred place. But in a handful of cases, I concluded that the person did not measure up to the criteria of being a sage as defined by Zalman Schachter-Shalomi. This was based on responses to questions, tone of voice, and my overall impression upon completion. Regardless, most of the interviews served to reinforce that the people interviewed are genuinely wise.

The themes that emerged from the sage and leader interviews informed the framework for the book. The chapters evolved from themes distilled after data analysis and represent the summation of what has been learned through the three relatively distinct learning processes of reviewing the literature, conducting the interviews, and training as a certified sage-ing leader. While individually the themes are not necessarily new to the leadership literature, viewing these concepts holistically is a new perspective. And the themes are based on more than 100 interviews with thought leaders—some of whom are no longer living. So I was able to capture their wisdom to pass onto others as legacy work.

*Living in More Than One World: How Peter Drucker's Wisdom Can Inspire and Transform Your Life* (2009) by Bruce Rosenstein is the most similar book I have discovered, but it is completely based on Drucker's thoughts about leadership and life; whereas my book is based on the life experiences and wisdom of more than 100 people— many of them recognized as significant thought leaders in the field.

## Additional Work

In addition to this research, there were several other activities that informed my thinking. First, there were workshops and seminars I attended, such as a leadership seminar as part of the Society for Organizational Learning (SoL) facilitated by Peter Senge from MIT, and a seminar on leadership at the Center for Creative Leadership (CCL) in Greensboro, North Carolina. Both of these experiences enabled me to interview people who might have been difficult to contact.

I attended a workshop at the Omega Institute in New York. The Omega Institute is one of the premier institutes with a mission of providing "innovative educational experiences that awaken the best in the human spirit and provides hope and healing for individuals and society." The workshop was a weekend with Pema Chödrön on

"Loving to Oneself and Merciful to Others." Pema Chödrön is an American Buddhist nun in the Shambhala Buddhist tradition and resident teacher at Gampo Abbey, a monastic center in Cape Breton, Nova Scotia. A student of Dzigar Kontrul Rinpoche, she is the author of several books.

In addition, I became certified as a Sage-ing Leader by Sage-ing International (www.sage-ing.org) founded by Rabbi Zalman Schachter-Shalomi, co-author of *From Age-ing to Sage-ing: A Profound New Vision of Growing Older* (1995). This groundbreaking work is the foundation for Sage-ing International. This certification allows me to conduct seminars using this information in ways that help people understand the value of harvesting life's wisdom. I am also certified as a Registered Corporate Coach focused on leadership development. This experience allows me to participate in personal coaching situations that help me to better understand the opportunities and challenges being faced by leaders in these uncertain times.

Another activity that informed my thinking was my involvement in a spiritual prayer group that was led by a certified spiritual director. This experience taught me about the best ways to lead discussions that encourage introspection and thoughtful reflection. The emphasis is on asking questions rather than having answers and it integrates silence as a tool for self-insight. Since sage-ing is spiritually based, this experience has helped me personally integrate these concepts.

Two other experiences taught me about leadership and change. First is my certification as a change management consultant with The Genysys Group. We help leaders initiate, lead, and sustain deep change. Another experience is my involvement with a faith-based community organizing group called AMOS (A Mid-Iowa Organizing

Strategy). AMOS is affiliated with the Industrial Areas Foundation (IAF) founded by Saul David Alinsky.

AMOS has been organizing within congregations and the community at large to help "re-weave" the social fabric of metropolitan Des Moines. AMOS is building an effort that is broad-based and cuts through the lines that divide us, such as race, socioeconomic status, geography and religious denomination; multi-issued, responding to a variety of concerns that are identified through intentional conversations in local congregations and communities; focused on the development of leaders in local congregations and communities; and seeking to exercise the power of organized people in a relational and responsible way. AMOS seeks out allies in the public and private sector to address the issues and concerns that affect the common good of the community.

When I was talking with Sherry Greenleaf, a certified leadership coach and one of my sages, she beautifully expressed the relationship between sage-ing and spirit at work: "Spirit at work is reaching back into our life experiences and pulling it into the present so that we can create the future. That activity is literally our spirit at work."

All of the activities mentioned above provide me with more life experiences to process into wisdom on my personal journey of becoming a sage. This has become my spirit at work.

# Appendix B

## About the Sages

Titles and affiliations were current at the time of the interview.

**Aburdene, Patricia:** One of the world's leading social forecasters. Co-author of *Megatrends* and *Megatrends 2010: The Rise of Conscious Capitalism.*

**Ackoff, Russ:** Anheuser-Busch professor emeritus of management science at the Wharton School, University of Pennsylvania. Author and co-author of 23 books with an emphasis in problem solving and systems thinking (deceased).

**Adson, Patricia:** Owner of Adson Coaching and Consulting, member of the leadership team at Hudson Institute of Santa Barbara.

**Anderson, Ray:** Founder and former CEO of Interface, Inc. and author of *Midcourse Correction Toward a Sustainable Enterprise: The Interface Model* and *Confessions of a Radical Industrialist: Profits, People, Purpose: Doing Business by Respecting the Earth* (deceased).

**Arrien, Angeles:** Cultural anthropologist and president of the Foundation for Cross-Cultural Education and Research. Author of *The Second Half of Life: Opening the Eight Gates of Wisdom* and *Living in Gratitude: A Journey That Will Change Your Life.*

**Atchley, Robert:** Distinguished professor emeritus of gerontology at Miami University, OH, where he also served as the director of the Scripps Gerontology Center. Author of *Social Forces and Aging* and of *Continuity and Adaptation in Aging: Creating Positive Experiences.*

***Autry, Jim:** Former president of the Magazine Group of Meredith Corporation, Des Moines, Iowa. Author of the classic *Love and Profit: The Art of Caring Leadership* and the more recent book *Choosing Gratitude: Learning to Love the Life You Have.*

**Backus, Robert "Skip":** Chief executive officer of Omega Institute. For more than 20 years, he has played a leadership role at Omega as operations director and campus manager, maintaining all of Omega's buildings. Backus has provided visionary leadership for the Omega Center for Sustainable Living (OCSL), an environmental education center and natural water reclamation facility.

**Bailey, Darlyne:** Dean and professor of the graduate school of social work and social research and special assistant to the president for community partnerships at Bryn Mawr College. Co-author of *Sustaining Our Spirits: Women Leaders Thriving for Today and Tomorrow.*

**Baldwin, Christina:** Co-founder of PeerSpirit, Inc., "a company focused on life and leadership through circle, quest, and story. Co-author of *The Circle Way: A Leader in Every Chair* and author of *Storycatcher: Making Sense of Our Lives Through the Power and Practice of Story.*

**Barrett, Richard:** Founder and chairman of the Values Centre. Creator of the internationally recognized Cultural Transformation Tools (CTT) and author of the books *Building a Values-Driven Organisation* and *Liberating the Corporate Soul.*

***Beck, Susan:** Director of organizational development at Hearthstone Homes, Omaha, Nebraska.

**Behar, Howard:** Former president of Starbucks Coffee International Inc. and author of *It's Not About the Coffee: Leadership Lessons from a Life at Starbucks.*

**\*\*Beizer, Barbara:** Founder of B2Works, a transition and organizational development firm.

**Benefiel, Margaret:** Executive officer of executive soul and author of *The Soul of a Leader.*

**Bennis, Warren:** Distinguished professor of business administration and founding chairman of The Leadership Institute at the University of Southern California. Author of *On Becoming a Leader: A Leadership Classic.*

**\*\*Biberman, Jerry:** Professor emeritus of management, department of management/marketing at the University of Scranton. Co-author of *At Work: Spirituality Matters.*

**Blair, Marilyn:** Owner of consulting firm TeamWork and former managing editor of OD Network publications.

**\*\*Block, Peter:** A partner in the firm Designed Learning; author of *Community: The Structure of Belonging* and co-author of *The Abundant Community: Awakening the Power of Families and Neighborhoods.*

**Bolman, Lee:** Professor and Marion Bloch/Missouri chair in leadership at the Bloch School of Business and Public Administration, University of Missouri-Kansas City. Co-author of *Leading with Soul: An Uncommon Journey of Spirit* and *Reframing Organizations: Artistry, Choice, and Leadership.*

**\*\*Boyatzis, Richard:** Professor in the departments of organizational behavior, psychology, and cognitive science at Case Western Reserve University and human resources at ESADE. Co-author of *Resonant Leadership* and *Becoming a Resonant Leader.*

**\*\*Bridges, William:** Founder of William Bridges and Associates. Author of *Managing Transitions: Making the Most of Change* and *The Way of Transition.*

**\*Brinkman, William:** Director of leadership formation at Ascension Health, Missouri, USA.

**\*Broccolo, Gerald:** Vice president of spirituality, Catholic Health Initiatives, Colorado, USA.

**Brown, Juanita:** Founder of Whole Systems Associates and co-originator of the World Café.

**\*\*Burack, Elmer:** Professor emeritus of management, University of Illinois at Chicago. Author of *Retiring Retirement: A New Roadmap for Longevity and Quality Living* (deceased).

**Cameron, Kim:** William Russell Kelly professor of management and organizations at the Ross School of Business at the University of Michigan. Author of *Positive Leadership: Strategies for Extraordinary Performance* and co-author of the book *Developing Managerial Skills.*

**Campbell, David:** Former executive vice president at the Center for Creative Leadership and creator of a leading career inventory, the Campbell Interest and Skills Survey (CISS). Author of *If You Don't Know Where You're Going, You'll Probably End Up Somewhere Else* and *If I'm in Charge Here, Why Is Everybody Laughing?*

**\*\*Carroll, Michael:** Owner of the consulting firm Awake at Work and author of *The Mindful Leader, Awake at Work,* and *Fearless at Work.*

**\*\*Cascio, Wayne:** Robert H. Reynolds Chair of Global Leadership Management, University of Colorado Denver and author of *Responsible Restructuring: Creative and Profitable Alternatives to Layoffs.*

**\*Clark, Lynn:** System executive with Memorial Hermann Healthcare System, Houston, Texas.

**\*\*Clawson, James:** Johnson & Higgins professor of business administration, the Darden Graduate School of Business University of Virginia and author of *Level Three Leadership: Getting Below the Surface.*

**Cohen, Allan:** Edward A. Madden distinguished professor of global leadership, Babson College and the co-author of *Managing for Excellence, Alternative Work Arrangements, Power Up: Transforming Organizations Through Shared Leadership*, and *Influence Without Authority.*

**Coombs, Ann:** Owner of Coombs Consulting and author of *The Living Workplace: Soul, Spirit, and Success in the 21ˢᵗ Century.*

**\*\*Coryell, Deborah M.:** Author of *Good Grief: Healing Through the Shadow of Loss.*

**Covey, Stephen:** Author of *The 7 Habits of Highly Effective People* and co-author of *First Things First* and *The Speed of Trust: The One Thing that Changes Everything* (deceased).

**Csikszentmihalyi, Mihaly:** Distinguished professor of psychology, director of the Quality of Life Research Center, Claremont Graduate School, The Drucker School. Author of *Flow: The Psychology of Optimal Experience* and *The Evolving Self.*

**Deal, Terrance:** The former Irving R. Meebo clinical professor of the Rossier School of Education at the University of Southern California. Co-author of *Leading With Soul: An Uncommon Journey of Spirit* and *Reframing Organizations: Artistry, Choice, and Leadership.*

**\*\*Delbecq, André:** The J. Thomas and Kathleen L. McCarthy University professor, management department, Leavey School of Business and Administration at Santa Clara University. Co-author of *Selected Readings in Management: Extensions and Modifications.*

**Dosher, Anne:** Elder with the Ashland Institute in Ashland, Oregon.

**De Pree, Max:** **Former CEO and** chairman of Herman Miller Corporation. Author of *Leadership Is an Art.*

*****Edwards, Julie:** CEO, Jesuit Social Services, Victoria, Australia.

**Fabor, Ann:** Executive coach, Center for Creative Leadership, North Carolina (deceased).

*****Fisher, Eileen:** Founder and CEO of Eileen Fisher, Inc.

**Flowers, Betty Sue:** Former director of the Lyndon Baines Johnson Library and Museum and an emeritus professor of English at the University of Texas at Austin. Co-author of *Presence: Human Purpose and the Field of the Future.*

**Freedman, Marc:** Founder and CEO of Encore.org, a nonprofit organization working to promote encore careers—second acts for the greater good. Author of *The Big Shift: Navigating the New Stage Beyond Midlife* and *Encore: Finding Work that Matters in the Second Half of Life.*

**Gallos, Joan:** Professor of leadership and University of Missouri Curators' distinguished teaching professor. Director, executive MBA program, Henry W. Bloch School of Business and Public Administration, University of Missouri-Kansas City. Author of *Business Leadership: A Jossey-Bass Reader* and co-author of *Reframing Organizations.*

**Goldman, Connie:** Former staff member of National Public Radio in Washington, DC., host of both daily and weekend broadcasts of NPR's *All Things Considered.* Author of *Who Am I … Now That I Am Not Who I Was* and *The Ageless Spirit: Reflections on Living Life to the Fullest in Midlife and the Years Beyond.*

**Goldsmith, Marshall:** Executive coach and co-author of *Coaching for Leadership: Writings on Leadership from the World's Greatest Coaches, What Got You Here Won't Get You There…in Sales,* and *Best Practices in Talent Management: How the World's Leading Corporations Manage, Develop, and Retain Top Talent.*

** **Greenleaf, Sherry:** Co-founder of IMPACT Training & Development, Inc.

**\*\*Hawk, Thomas:** Professor emeritus, Frostburg University.

**Heerman, Barry:** Creator of the Noble Purpose Program and the Team Spirit Team Development Program offered by the Plexus Corporation. Author of *Building Team Spirit: Activities for Inspiring and Energizing Teams.*

**\*\*Helgesen, Sally:** Author of *The Female Vision: Women's Real Power at Work* and the classic book on women's leadership styles *The Female Advantage: Women's Ways of Leadership.*

**\*Hellmich, Philip:** Co-director of Individual Giving, Search for Common Ground, United States and Worldwide, Washington, DC.

**\*Herl, Tamera:** Director of expressive therapies at Prairie View Inc., Kansas.

**\*Hodgson, Judy:** Senior vice president, organizational development, PeaceHealth, Washington, USA.

**Hunter, James:** Founder of J.D. Hunter and Associates and author of *The Servant: The Simple Story About the Essence of Leadership.*

**Jons, Carolyn:** Life and organizational coach from the Hudson Institute, Ames, Iowa.

**Kellerman, Barbara:** The James MacGregor Burns lecturer in public leadership at Harvard University's John F. Kennedy School of Government. Founding executive director of the Kennedy Schools Center for Public Leadership. Author of *Bad Leadership, Followership,* and *The End of Leadership.*

**Koestenbaum, Peter:** Founder and chairman of PiB and the Koestenbaum Institute. Author of *Leadership: The Inner Side of Greatness.*

**Kouzes, Jim:** Dean's executive professor of leadership, Leavey School of Business, at Santa Clara University; and co-author of *Encouraging the Heart: How Leaders Can Inspire Others for Consistently*

*Extraordinary Performance, The Leadership Challenge: How to Make Extraordinary Things Happen in Organizations,* and *A Leader's Legacy.*

**\*\*Leider, Richard:** Founder of the Inventure Group and author of *The Power of Purpose, Claiming Your Place at the Fire: Living the Second Half of Your Life on Purpose,* and *Something to Live For: Finding Your Way in the Second Half of Life.*

**\*\*Lincoln, Yvonna:** Distinguished professor of higher education and educational administration and human resource development, Texas A&M University. Co-author of *Naturalistic Inquiry* and co-editor of *Handbook of Qualitative Research.*

**\*Maddix, Thomas:** Vice president of mission, ethics, and spirituality of Providence Health Care in Vancouver, British Columbia.

**\*Mahjoor, Fasha:** Founder and president, Phenomenex, Torrance, California.

**Marcic, Dorothy:** Former professor at Vanderbilt University's Owen Graduate School of Management and former director of graduate programs in human resource development. Co-author of *Understanding Management* and author of *Managing with Wisdom and Love: Uncovering Virtue in People and Organizations.*

**\*\*Marx, Robert:** Professor of management, Isenberg School of Management, University of Massachusetts—Amherst. Co-editor of *The Virtuous Organization: Insights From Some of the World's Leading Management Thinkers.*

**Mitchell, P. J.:** Vice president, global sales and operations, IBM Corporation.

**\*\*Moody, Harry "Rick":** Director of academic affairs for AARP and former chairman of the board of Elderhostel (now Road Scholar). Author of *Five Stages of the Soul.*

**Moxley, Russ:** President of Moxley & Associates and former fellow at the Center for Creative Leadership. Author of *Leadership and Spirit: Breathing New Vitality and Energy into Individuals and Organizations.*

\*\***Neal, Judi:** Founder of the Tyson Center for Faith and Spirituality in the Workplace at the University of Arkansas—formerly known as the International Center for Spirit at Work and author of *Edgewalkers: People and Organizations That Take Risks, Build Bridges, and Break New Ground.*

**Noer, David:** President of Noer Consulting and author of *Healing the Wounds: Overcoming the Trauma of Layoffs and Revitalizing Downsized Organizations.*

**Olson, Doug:** Chief risk officer at GreatAmerica Leasing Corporation in Cedar Rapids, Iowa.

\*\***Ouimet, J.-Robert:** Chairman of the board and chief executive officer of Holding O.C.B. Inc., Cordon Bleu International Ltd., and of Piazza Tomasso International Inc.

**Palmer, Parker:** Founder and senior partner of the Center for Courage & Renewal. Author of *Let Your life Speak: Listening for the Voice of Vocation.*

\*\***Petersen, Dan:** Executive coach and owner of Open Focus in Sage Canyon, Colorado.

**Pink, Daniel:** Author of *A Whole New Mind: Why Right-Brainers Will Rule the Future* and *Drive: The Surprising Truth About What Motivates Us.*

\***Piramal, Swati:** Director, Nicholas Piramal India, Ltd., Mumbai, India.

\*\***Radia, Suku:** CEO of Bankers Trust, Des Moines, Iowa.

**Renesch, John:** Member of the practitioner faculty for the Center for Leadership Studies and former publisher and editor-in-chief of New Leaders Press. Author of *The Great Growing Up.*

**Richo, David:** Author of *Coming Home to Who You Are  Discovering Your Natural Capacity for Love, Integrity, and Compassion* and *Shadow Dance: Liberating the Power & Creativity of Your Dark Side.*

**Roy, Peter:** Founder and former president of Whole Foods, Inc. Co-author of *The Book of Hard Choices.*

**\*Sartori, Beth:** Director of corporate communications, Memorial Hermann Healthcare System, Houston, Texas.

**Schachter-Shalomi, Zalman:** Rabbi and founder of Spiritual Eldering Institute (now Sage-ing International), co-author of *From Ageing to Sage-ing: A Profound New Vision of Growing Older.*

**Seashore, Edith:** Former president of NTL Institute, co-founder of the American University/NTL Institute master's program in OD, and also co-founder of The Lewin Center. Author of *Triple Impact Coaching: Use of Self in the Coaching Process.*

**Senge, Peter:** Senior lecturer at the Massachusetts Institute of Technology and founding chair of the Society for Organizational Learning (SoL). Author of the classic book *The Fifth Discipline: The Art and Practice of the Learning Organization* and co-author of *Presence: Human Purpose and the Field of the Future.*

**Seymour, Daniel:** Author of *Once Upon a Campus: Lessons for Improving Quality and Productivity in Higher Education* and *On Q: Causing Quality in Higher Education.*

**\*Shors, Susan:** Chief culture office, Eileen Fisher, Inc.

**\*Simon, Tami:** CEO, Sounds True, Littleton, Colorado.

**\*Smith, John:** President and CEO, Hearthstone Homes, Omaha, Nebraska

**\*Stoltenberg, Jessica:** Vice president of public relations, Medtronic, Inc., Minneapolis, Minnesota.

**Thomas, William:** Founder of the Eden Alternative and Green House Project and author of the book *What Are Old People For? How Elders Will Save The World.*

**Thompson, C. Michael:** Author of *The Congruent Life: Following the Inward Path to Fulfilling Work and Inspired Leadership*

**Vaill, Peter:** University professor of management at Antioch University and author of *Learning as a Way of Being: Strategies for Survival in a World of Permanent White Water* and *Spirited Leading and Learning: Process Wisdom for a New Age.*

*\*VanDuivendyk, Tim:* Memorial Hermann Healthcare System, Houston, Texas

**Weiner, Edith:** President of Weiner, Edrich, Brown, Incorporated and co-author of *FutureThink: How to Think Clearly in a Time of Change.*

\*\* **Wharff, Jonah:** Trappist-Cistercian monk at New Melleray Abbey in Dubuque, Iowa.

\*\* **Wheatley, Margaret:** Co-founder and president emerita of The Berkana Institute, author of *Leadership and the New Science: Discovering Order in a Chaotic World,* and *Turning to One Another: Simple Conversations to Restore Hope to the Future.*

**Whetten, David:** The Jack Wheatley professor of organizational studies and director of the faculty development center at Brigham Young University. Co-author of *Developing Managerial Skills.*

**Whiteley, Richard:** Vice chairman and co-founder of The Forum Corporation. Author *of The Customer-Driven Company.*

\*\***Wimer, Connie:** Owner and CEO of Business Publications Incorporated, Des Moines, Iowa.

\*Yahraes, Sefina:** Assistant of management, Clean ServicePower Gmbh, Bonn, Germany.

**Zuboff, Shoshana:** Former Charles Edward Wilson Professor of Business Administration at Harvard Business School and co-author of *The Support Economy: Why Corporations Are Failing Individuals and the Next Episode of Capitalism.*

*Interviewees from award-winning organizations
**Multiple interviews and/or ongoing conversations

# References

Albom, M. (1997). *Tuesdays With Morrie: An Old Man, A Young Man and Life's Greatest Lesson.* New York: Doubleday.

Anderson, R. (1999). *Mid-Course Correction: Toward a Sustainable Enterprise, The Interface Model.* Atlanta, GA: Peregrinzilla Press.

Autry, J.A. (1991). *Love and Profit: The Art of Caring Leadership.* New York: William Morrow and Company.

Autry, J.A. (2001). *The Servant Leader: How to Build a Creative Team, Develop Great Morale, and Improve Bottom-line Performance.* New York: Three Rivers Press.

Autry, J.A. (2012). *Choosing Gratitude: Learning to Love the Life You Have.* Macon, GA: Smyth & Helwys Publishing, Inc.

Arrien, A. (2011). *Living in Gratitude: A Journal That Will Change Your Life.* Boulder, CO: Sounds True, Inc.

Bailey, D., K.M. Koney, M.E. McNish, R. Powers, R., and K. Uhly. (2008). *Sustaining Our Spirits: Women Leaders Thriving for Today and Tomorrow.* Washington, DC: National Association of Social Workers.

Baldwin, C. (2005). *Storycatcher: Making Sense of Our Lives Through the Power and Practice of Story.* Novato, CA: New World Library.

Baldwin, C. (2010). *The Circle Way: A Leader in Every Chair.* San Francisco: Berrett-Koehler Publishers.

Bateson, M.C. (1989). *Composing a Life.* New York: Grove/Atlantic, Inc.

Beck, R. and S.B. Metrick. (1990). *The Art of Ritual: A Guide to Creating and Performing Your Own Rituals for Growth and Change.* Berkeley, CA: Celestial Arts.

Behar, H. (2007). *It's Not About the Coffee: Leadership Lessons from a Life at Starbucks.* New York: Penguin Group, Inc.

Block, P. (2008). *Community: The Structure of Belonging.* San Francisco: Berrett-Koehler Publishers, Inc.

Boyatzis, R. and A. McKee. (2005). *Resonant Leadership: Renewing Ourself and Connecting With Others Through Mindfulness, Hope, and Compassion.* Boston: Harvard Business School Press.

Bridges, W. (2001). *The Way of Transition.* New York: Perseus Publishing Services.

Brown, B. (2012*). Daring Greatly: How the Courage to Be Vulnerable Transforms the Way We Live, Love, Parent, and Lead.* New York: Gotham Books.

Brown, M. (1947). *Stone Soup.* New York: Atheneum Books.

Bryant, A. (2011). *The Corner Office: Indispensable and Unexpected Lessons from CEOs on How to Lead and Succeed.* New York: Times Books.

Bryant, J.H. (2009). *Love Leadership: The New Way to Lead in a Fear-Based World.* San Francisco: Jossey-Bass.

Buechner, F. (1973). *Wishful Thinking: A Theological ABC.* New York: HarperOne.

Cameron, J. (2007). *The Complete Artist's Way: Creativity as a Spiritual Practice.* New York: The Penguin Group.

Cameron, K. (2012). *Positive Leadership: Strategies for Extraordinary Performance.* San Francisco: Berrett-Koehler Publishers, Inc.

Cameron, K.S. and R.E. Quinn. (1999). "An Introduction to Changing Organizational Culture." In *Diagnosing and Changing Organizational Culture,* (pp. 1-17). Reading, MA: Addison-Wesley.

CareerBliss. (December 9, 2012). "CareerBliss 50 Happiest Companies in America for 2013." CareerBliss, http://www.careerbliss.com/facts-and-figures/careerbliss-50-happiest-companies-in-america-for-2013/.

Carroll, M. (2007). *The Mindful Leader: Awakening Your Natural Management Skills Through Mindfulness Meditation.* Boston: Trumpeter.

Carroll, M. (2004). *Awake at Work: 35 Practical Buddhist Principles for Discovering Clarity and Balance in the Midst of Work's Chaos.* Boston: Shambhala Publications, Inc.

Carroll, M. (2012a). *Fearless at Work: Timeless Teachings for Awakening Confidence, Resilience, and Creativity in the Face of Life's Demands.* Boston: Shambhala Publications, Inc.

Carroll, M. (2012b). "Lead By Achieving Nothing. Seriously." *Forbes,* http://www.forbes.com/sites/forbesleadershipforum/2012/11/16/lead-by-achieving-nothing-seriously/print.

Cebuhar, J.K. (2010). *So Grows the Tree—Creating an Ethical Will—The Legacy of Your Beliefs and Values, Life Lessons and Hopes for the Future.* Des Moines, IA: Murphy Publishing.

Chodran, P. (2005). *The Places that Scare You: A Guide to Fearlessness in Difficult Times.* Boston: Shambhala Publications, Inc.

Collins, J. (March, 1999). "The Learning Person." *Training,* 84.

Collins, J. (2001). *Good to Great: Why Some Companies Make the Leap...and Others Don't.* New York: HarperCollins Publishing, Inc.

Collins, J. (2011). *Great by Choice: Uncertainty, Chaos, and Luck—Why Some Thrive Despite Them All.* New York: HarperCollins Publishing, Inc.

Coombs, A. (2004). *The Living Workplace: Soul, Spirit, and Success in the 21st Century.* Toronto: Warwick Publishing, Inc.

Coryell, D.M. (2007). *Good Grief: Healing Through the Shadow of Loss.* Rochester, Vermont: Healing Arts Press.

Coutu, D.L. (2002). "How Resilience Works." *Harvard Business Review,* 80(5), 46-50, 52, 55.

Covey, S.R. (2004). *Seven Habits of Highly Effective People.* New York: Free Press.

Covey, S.R. and R. Merrill.(2006). *The Speed of Trust: The One Thing that Changes Everything.* New York: Free Press.

Covey, S.R., A.R. Merrill, and R.R. Merrill. (1994). *First Things First.* New York: Fireside.

Csikszentmihalyi, M. (1994). *The Evolving Self: A Psychology for the Third Millennium.* New York: HarperCollins Publisher, Inc.

de Saint-Exupery, A. (1943). *The Little Prince.* Orlando, Florida: Harcourt, Inc.

Delbecq A. (2009). "Spirituality and Business: One Scholar's Perspective." *Journal of Management, Spirituality and Religion,* 6(1), 3-13.

Delbecq, A. (2011). "'Evil' Manifested in Destructive Individual Behavior: A Senior Leadership Challenge." *Journal of Management Inquiry,* 10(3), 221-226.

Delbecq, A. (2012). "Spiritual Practices for the Leader." Working Paper, p. 9.

Dewan, S. (2006). "Amish School Survivors Struggle After Killings." *New York Times,* October 5.

Dishman, L. (2013). "Secrets of America's Happiest Companies."

Fast Company, www.fastcompany.com/3004595/secrest-americas-happiest-companies.

Freedman, M. (2011). *The Big Shift: Navigating the New Stage Beyond Midlife.* New York: Public Affairs.

Frost, P.J. (2003). *Toxic Emotions at Work: How Compassionate Managers Handle Pain and Conflict.* Boston: Harvard Business School Press.

Frost, P.J. (2007). *Toxic Emotions at Work: And What You Can Do About Them.* Boston: Harvard Business School Press.

Galford, R. and R. Maruca. (2006). *Your Leadership Legacy: Why Looking Toward the Future Will Make You a Better Leader Today.* Boston, MA: Harvard Business School Publishing.

Gallup Organization. (2013). "The High Cost of Disengaged Employees." *Gallup Business Journal,* http://businessjournal.gallup.com/content/247/the-high-cost-of-disengaged-employees.aspx.

Gardner, J. W. (1990). *On Leadership.* New York: The Free Press.

Gibb, J.R. (1978). *Trust.* Los Angeles: Guild of Tutors Press.

Giono, J. (1996). *The Man Who Planted Trees.* London: Owen (Peter) Ltd.

Gladwell, M. (2008). *Outliers: The Story of Success.* New York: Little, Brown & Company.

Glaser, B.G., and A.L. Strauss. (1967). *The Discovery of Grounded Theory: Strategies for Qualitative Research.* Chicago: Aldine.

Goleman, D. (1995). *Emotional Intelligence: Why It Can Matter More Than IQ.* New York: Bantom Books.

Greenleaf, R. (2002). *Servant Leadership: A Journey into the Nature of Legitimate Power and Greatness* (L.C. Spears, Ed.). New Jersey: Paulist Press.

Hazen, M.A. (2008). "Grief and the Workplace." *Academy of Management Perspectives,* 22(3), 78-86.

Heath, D., and C. Heath. (2007). *Made to Stick: Why Some Ideas Survive and Others Die.* New York: Random House.

Heifetz, R.A., and M. Linksy. (2002). *Leadership on the Line: Staying Alive Through the Dangers of Leading.* Boston: Harvard Business School.

Heifetz, R.A., and D.L. Laurie. (1997, January/February). "The Work of Leadership." *Harvard Business Review* 75(1), 124-134.

Hesselbein, F. (2011). *My Life in Leadership: The Journey and Lessons Learned Along the Way.* San Francisco, CA: Jossey-Bass.

Isay, D. (2007). *Listening Is an Act of Love.* New York: The Penguin Press.

Isenberg, S., L. Iser, and B. Sugarman. (2006). *The Sage-ing Workbook.* Bloomington, IN: The Sage-ing Guild.

James, J.W., and R. Friedman. (2003). "Grief Index: The 'Hidden' Annual Costs of Grief in America's Workplace." The Grief Recovery Institute Educational Foundation, Inc., www.grief-recovery.com/request_index.htm.

Jobs, S. (2005). "Stay Hungry. Stay Foolish." *Fortune,* September 5, 31-32.

Jones, D. (2009, March 10). "How Cheating Death Can Change Your Life." *USA Today,* 1-2B.

Kabat-Zinn, J. (2000). *Wherever You Go, There You Are.* New York: Hyperion.

Kanter, R.M. (2005). "Get Involved—You'll Be Happy That You Did." *Miami Herald,* October 6.

Kellerman, B. (2004). *Bad Leadership: What It Is, How It Happens, Why It Matters.* Boston: Harvard Business School Press.

Kelly, M., and P. Lencioni. (2007). *The Dream Manager.* New York: Beacon Publishing.

Kerr, S. (1995). "On the Folly of Rewarding A While Hoping for B." *The Academy of Management Executive,* 9(1), 7-14.

Kim, W.C., and R.A. Mauborgne. (July-August, 1992). "Parables of Leadership." *Harvard Business Review,* 123-128.

Kouzes, J.M., B.Z. Posner. (2006). *A Leader's Legacy.* San Francisco: John Wiley & Sons, Inc.

Kouzes, J.M., and B.Z. Posner. (1999). *Encouraging the Heart: How Leaders Can Inspire Others for Consistently Extraordinary Performance.* San Francisco: Jossey-Bass.

Kouzes, J.M., and B Z. Posner. (2012). *Leadership Challenge: How to Make Extraordinary Things Happen in Organizations.* San Francisco: Jossey-Bass.

Kraybill, D.B., S.M. Nolt, and D.L. Weaver-Zercher. (2007). *Amish Grace: How Forgiveness Transcended Tragedy.* San Francisco: Jossey-Bass.

Lamott, A. (1999). *Traveling Mercies: Some Thoughts on Faith.* New York: Anchor Books.

La Monica, P.R. (January, 2010). "Best Places to Work: No Stock? No Problem," http://money.cnn.com/2010/01/26/markets/thebuzz/.

Langer, E.J. (2009). *Counterclockwise: Mindful Health and the Power of Possibility.* New York: Ballentine Books.

Langer, E.J. (1997). *The Power of Mindful Learning.* New York: Perseus Books.

Langer, E.J. (1989). *Mindfulness.* New York: Perseus Books.

Lawrence, P.R., and N. Nohria. (2002). *Driven: How Human Nature Shapes our Choices.* San Francisco: Jossey-Bass.

Leider, R.J. (2012). *The Power of Purpose.* San Francisco: Berrett-Koehler Publishers, Inc.

Leider, R.J. (2009). "Discovering What Matters: Balancing Money, Medicine, and Meaning." MetLife Mature Life Institute, www.metlife.com/assets/cao/mmi/publications/studies/mmi-discovering-what-matters-study.pdf.

Leider, R.J., and D.A. Shapiro. (2004). *Claiming Your Place at the Fire: Living the Second Half of Your Life on Purpose.* San Francisco: Berrett-Koehler Publishers, Inc.

Leider, R.J., and D.A. Shapiro. (2008). *Something to Live For: Finding Your Way in the Second Half of Life.* San Francisco: Berrett-Koehler Publishers, Inc.

Lincoln, Y S., and E.G. Guba. (1985). *Naturalistic Inquiry.* Newbury Park, CA: Sage Publications.

Luskin, F. (2002). *Forgive for Good: A Proven Prescription for Health and Happiness.* New York: HarperCollins Publishers.

McKee, A., R. Boyatzis, and F. Johnston. (2008). *Becoming a Resonant Leader: Develop Your Emotional Intelligence, Renew Your Relationships, and Sustain Your Effectiveness.* Boston: Harvard Business School Publishing.(2008)

McKee, A., Johnston, F. and Massimilian, R. (2006). "Mindfulness, Hope and Compassion: A Leader's Road Map to Renewal." *Ivy Business Journal,* 1-6.

McKnight, J., and P. Block. (2010). *The Abundant Community: Awakening the Power of Families and Neighborhoods.* San Francisco: Berrett-Koehler.

McPhearson, M., L. Smith-Lovin, and M.E. Brashears. (2006). "Social Isolation in America: Changes in Core Discussion Networks Over Two Decades." *American Sociological Review,* 71(June), 353-375.

MetLife Mature Market Institute (January, 2009). "Discovering What Matters: Balancing Money, Medicine, and Meaning." Westport, CT: MetLife Mature Market Institute, www.metlife.com/assets/cao/mmi/publications/studies/mmi-discovering-what-matters-study.pdf

Meyer, D. (2006). *Setting the Table: The Transforming Power of Hospitality in Business.* New York: HarperCollins Publishers.

Moxley, R.S. (2000). *Leadership and Spirit: Breathing New Vitality and Energy into Individuals and Organizations.* San Francisco: Jossey-Bass.

Noer, D.M. (1993). *Healing the Wounds: Overcoming the Trauma of Layoffs and Revitalizing Downsized Organizations.* San Francisco: Jossey-Bass Inc.

O'Neil, J.R. (1993). *The Paradox of Success: When Winning at Work Means Losing at Life*. New York: G.P. Putnam's Sons.

Overton, P. (1997). *Re-building the Front Porch of America: Essays on the Art of Community Making*. Columbia, MO: Columbia College.

Palmer, P. (2000). *Let Your Life Speak: Listening for the Voice of Vocation*. San Francisco: Jossey-Bass Inc.

Parrish, B. (2007). *Wise Woman's Way: A Guide to Growing Older with Purpose and Passion*. Morro Bay, CA: Morro Press.

Pirsig, R. (1974). *Zen and the Art of Motorcycle Maintenance*. New York: Bantam Books.

Pfeffer, J. (1998). *The Human Equation: Building Profits by Putting People First*. Boston: Harvard Business School Press.

Putnam, R.D., and L.M. Feldstein. (2003). *Better Together: Restoring the American Community*. New York: Simon & Schuster.

Putnam, R.D. (2000). *Bowling Alone: The Collapse and Revival of American Community*. New York: Simon and Schuster.

Quindlen, A. (2000). *A Short Guide to a Happy Life*. New York: Random House.

Quinn, D. (1992). *Ishmael: An Adventure of the Mind and Spirit*. New York: Bantam Books.

Radia, S. (2010). "Iowans' Concern for Others Is Powerful." *Des Moines Register*, 11A.

Richo, D. (1999). *Shadow Dance: Liberating the Power & Creativity of Your Dark Side*. Boston: Shambhala.

Rosenstein, B. (2009). *Living in More Than One World: How Peter Drucker's Wisdom Can Inspire and Transform Your Life*. San Francisco: Berrett-Koehler Publishers, Inc.

Schachter-Shalomi, Z., and Miller, R.S. (1995). *From Age-ing to Sage-ing: A Profound New Vision of Growing Older*. New York: Warner Books.

Senge, P. (1990). *The Fifth Discipline: The Art and Practice of the Learning Organization.* New York: Doubleday/Currency.

Senge, P., C.O. Scharmer, J. Jaworski, and B.S. Flowers. (2004). *Presence: Human Purpose and the Field of the Future.* Cambridge, MA: The Society for Organizational Learning.

Slater, P. (1976). *The Pursuit of Loneliness. American Culture at the Breaking Point.* Boston: Beacon Press.

Stewart, T.A. (September 7, 1998). "The Cunning Plots of Leadership." *Fortune*, 165-166.

Strauss, A.C., and J.M. Corbin. (1990). *Basics of Qualitative Research: Grounded Theory Procedures and Techniques.* Thousand Oaks, CA: Sage Publications.

Snyder, S. (2013). *Leadership and the Art of Struggle.* San Francisco: Berrett-Koehler Publishers.

Sutton, R.I. (2010). *Good Boss, Bad Boss: How to Be the Best… and Learn from the Worst.* New York: Hachette Book Group.

Taylor, M. (2008). *DailyOM: Inspirational Thoughts for a Happy, Healthy, and Fulfilling Day.* Carlsbad, CA: Hay House, Inc.

Taylor, M. (2010). *DailyOM: Learning to Live.* Carlsbad, CA: Hay House, Inc.

Tolle, E. (1999). *The Power of Now: A Guide to Spiritual Awakening.* Vancouver, Canada: Namaste Publishing.

Tolle, E. (2003). *Stillness Speaks.* Vancouver, Canada: Namaste Publishing.

Tolle, E. (2005). *A New Earth: Awakening to Your Life's Purpose.* New York: Penguin Group.

Wallace, D. F. (2009). *This Is Water: Some Thoughts, Delivered on a Significant Occasion, About Living a Compassionate Life.* New York: Little, Brown and Company.

Warren, R. (2002). *The Purpose Driven Life: What on Earth am I Here For?* Grand Rapids, MI: Zondervan.

Weick, K.E. (1984). "Small Wins: Redefining the Scale of Social Problems." *American Psychologist,* 29(1), 40-49.

Wheatley, M.J. (1999). *Leadership and the New Science: Discovering Order in a Chaotic World.* San Francisco: Berrett-Koehler Publishers, Inc.

Wheatley, M.J. (2009). *Turning to One Another: Simple Conversations to Restore Hope to the Future.* San Francisco: Berrett-Koehler Publishers, Inc.

Whetten, D.A., and K.S. Cameron. (2011). *Developing Management Skills.* Upper Saddle River, NJ: Pearson Prentice Hall.

# About the Author

Jann Freed is a Leadership Development and Change Management Consultant with The Genysys Group. She primarily works with individuals and businesses in the Midwest to transition—to get from where they are to where they want to be. She has worked with companies such as Wells Fargo, Principal Financial Group, Vermeer Manufacturing, Nationwide, and Meredith Corporation.

She is professor emerita of business management and the former Mark and Kay De Cook Endowed Chair in Leadership and Character Development at Central College in Pella, Iowa where she joined the faculty in 1981. She earned her PhD from Iowa State University, MBA at Drake University, and undergraduate degree in business management from Central College.

She is the co-author of four books—three on continuous improvement in higher education and one on learner-centered assessment on college campuses: *Learner-Centered Assessment on College Campuses: Shifting the Focus from Teaching to Learning* (Pearson, 1999) *Quality Principles And Practices In Higher Education: Different Questions For Different Times* (American Council on Education and Oryx Press, 1997), and *A Culture for Academic Excellence: Implementing the Quality Principles in Higher Education* (George Washington University, 1997). Her last book, *Women of Yucatan: Thirty Who Dare To Change Their World* (McFarland Publishing, 2009) was on Mexican women leaders that evolved out of a cross-cultural research and teaching experience. Jann can be reached at JannFreed@JannFreed.com.

# Index

# Index

# Index

# HOW TO PURCHASE ASTD PRESS PRODUCTS

All ASTD Press titles may be purchased through ASTD's online store at **www.store.astd.org**.

ASTD Press products are available worldwide through various outlets and booksellers. In the United States and Canada, individuals may also purchase titles (print or eBook) from:

**Amazon**– www.amazon.com (USA); www.amazon.com (CA)
**Google Play**– play.google.com/store
**EBSCO**– www.ebscohost.com/ebooks/home

Outside the United States, English-language ASTD Press titles may be purchased through distributors (divided geographically).

**United Kingdom, Continental Europe, the Middle East, North Africa, Central Asia, and Latin America:**
Eurospan Group
Phone: 44.1767.604.972
Fax: 44.1767.601.640
Email: eurospan@turpin-distribution.com
Web: www.eurospanbookstore.com
For a complete list of countries serviced via Eurospan please visit www.store.astd.org or email publications@astd.org.

**South Africa:**
Knowledge Resources
Phone: +27(11)880-8540
Fax: +27(11)880-8700/9829
Email: mail@knowres.co.za
Web: http://www.kr.co.za
For a complete list of countries serviced via Knowledge Resources please visit www.store.astd.org or email publications@astd.org.

**Nigeria:**
Paradise Bookshops
Phone: 08033075133
Email: paradisebookshops@gmail.com
Website: www.paradisebookshops.com

**Asia:**
Cengage Learning Asia Pte. Ltd.
Email: asia.info@cengage.com
Web: www.cengageasia.com
For a complete list of countries serviced via Cengage Learning please visit www.store.astd.org or email publications@astd.org.

**India:**
Cengage India Pvt. Ltd.
Phone: 011 43644 1111
Fax: 011 4364 1100
Email: asia.infoindia@cengage.com

For all other countries, customers may send their publication orders directly to ASTD. Please visit: **www.store.astd.org**.